Famous Flyers

Claire Chennault
Amelia Earhart
Charles Lindbergh
Eddie Rickenbacker
Manfred von Richthofen
Chuck Yeager

Famous Flyers

Amelia Earhart

Heather Lehr Wagner

CHELSEA HOUSE
PUBLISHERS
A Haights Cross Communications Company
Philadelphia

Frontis: The contributions Amelia Earhart made to aviation extend beyond her records and milestones. Her accomplishments inspired young women to fly more, to fly faster, and to fly better.

CHELSEA HOUSE PUBLISHERS

VP, NEW PRODUCT DEVELOPMENT Sally Cheney
DIRECTOR OF PRODUCTION Kim Shinners
CREATIVE MANAGER Takeshi Takahashi
MANUFACTURING MANAGER Diann Grasse

Staff for AMELIA EARHART

EXECUTIVE EDITOR Lee Marcott
ASSOCIATE EDITOR Bill Conn
PRODUCTION EDITOR Jaimie Winkler
PHOTO EDITOR Sarah Bloom
COVER AND SERIES DESIGNER Keith Trego
LAYOUT 21st Century Publishing and Communications, Inc.

A Haights Cross Communications ✈ Company

http://www.chelseahouse.com

First Printing

1 3 5 7 9 8 6 4 2

Library of Congress Cataloging-in-Publication Data

Wagner, Heather Lehr.
  Amelia Earhart / Heather Lehr Wagner.
    v. cm. -- (Famous flyers)
Includes index.
Contents: The first adventure -- The feeling of flying -- A new career
-- Solo across the Atlantic -- The Pacific challenge -- Around the world
-- Into the stars.
  ISBN 0-7910-7213-4 (Hardcover) -- ISBN 0-7910-7498-6 (Paperback) 1. Earhart,
Amelia, 1897-1937--Juvenile literature. 2. Air pilots--United States--Biography--
Juvenile literature. 3. Women air pilots--United States--Biography--Juvenile litera-
ture. [1. Earhart, Amelia, 1897-1937. 2. Air pilots. 3. Women--Biography.] I. Title. II.
Series.
  TL540.E3 W34 2003
  629.13'092--dc21

2002155104

CONTENTS

The First Adventure

On the morning of June 17, 1928, an orange Fokker F7 airplane took off from Trepassey in Newfoundland. Its crew had arrived from Boston more than 12 days earlier and had been waiting for the right weather conditions to permit them to set off on the second stage of their trip. The airplane, named the *Friendship*, had been designed to fly over land, but more recently its wheels had been exchanged for pontoons to enable it to take off and land on water.

Day after day of fog and rain had stranded the crew at Trepassey, and they had spent the time making adjustments to their plane, playing cards, and trying to enjoy sightseeing in the cold and damp weather. The crew had only one map to study, and they carefully examined the passage of storms and weather systems across their charted journey until finally conditions made it seem possible that they could complete their trip—a trip that would take them across the Atlantic Ocean. One year earlier, Charles Lindbergh had made history by becoming the first man to fly across the Atlantic. Since his extraordinary flight, 26 men had made six successful trips across the ocean.

But the *Friendship* would be making its own history, if it could successfully complete its journey across the Atlantic. It would add two more men to the roster of those who had completed the transatlantic flight, plus one woman—a young aviator named Amelia Earhart.

Amelia Earhart smiles in triumph as she arrives in Southampton, England, on June 26, 1928, following a grueling flight that started in Newfoundland. This flight made her the first woman to fly across the Atlantic Ocean.

ACROSS THE ATLANTIC

The flight had been arranged by Amy Guest, a wealthy socialite, who had hoped to make the trip herself. But the journey was extremely risky, and Guest's family had refused to allow her to attempt the crossing. She chose in her place a 30-year-old social worker from Boston who was known for her skills as an amateur pilot, a woman named Amelia Earhart.

Earhart was slim, with short brown hair and bright blue eyes. Many who met her were amazed at her resemblance to Lindbergh, and as part of the publicity campaign surrounding the flight she was labeled "Lady Lindy."

There were other women attempting to be the first to fly across the Atlantic, so the crew of the *Friendship* was under intense pressure to make their flight as quickly as possible. Until their departure from Boston on the first part of the journey, their plans had been kept a secret. Even Amelia's own family was unaware of her effort to be the first woman across the Atlantic. The flight was hazardous—many had tried to make the crossing and, lacking the proper navigation skills or equipment or suffering from exhaustion after nearly 24 hours of straight flying, had failed.

Amelia left behind letters for her family, to be opened in the event that the plane crashed. To her sister Muriel, she noted, "If I succeed all will be well. If I don't, I shall be happy to pop off in the midst of such an adventure." Her mother's letter contained the reassurance, "My life has really been very happy," while Amelia's message to her father demonstrated a true reflection of her excitement at the prospect of the trip: "Hooray for the last grand adventure!"

Amelia's preparations for her historic flight were fairly simple. Her only luggage was a small knapsack containing the bare essentials—a comb, a toothbrush, two handkerchiefs, and a small container of cream. To record the details of the trip she carried a pair of binoculars, a camera, and a small journal.

While most of the attention, both before and after the trip, would fall on Amelia, the crew of three also included two experienced aviators whose skills would prove critical to the safety of the flight. Although Amelia was a trained aviator, she would do none of the actual flying. Wilmer "Bill" Stultz was the pilot, a 28-year-old flyer who had served in both the army and navy air forces. Louis Edward "Slim" Gordon—a 27-year-old veteran of the army's air force—served as copilot and mechanic.

The first leg of the journey created great publicity for

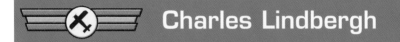

Charles Lindbergh

On May 20, 1927, a young airmail pilot took off from a rainy airstrip on Long Island. He would fly alone across the Atlantic for 33 and one-half hours before landing in Paris to a cheering crowd, welcoming the first person to fly across the Atlantic Ocean.

Lindbergh's flight—in a small monoplane dubbed the *Spirit of St. Louis*, which he had configured himself—transformed aviation. An international audience had followed his daring flight and celebrated when he arrived safely. With the success of his transatlantic journey, the airplane suddenly seemed more than a vehicle for stunts and daredevil pilots—it was a resource for a new commercial field, the field of aviation.

Lindbergh wrote a book about his flight, titled *We*, that was an instant bestseller. He continued to contribute to aviation, conducting surveying flights to Europe, Asia, Africa, Greenland, and South America for Pan American Airways. He served as a technical adviser for Transcontinental Air Transport (which would become TWA), one of the earliest commercial airlines. He also assisted in efforts to fund research by Robert H. Goddard that would become critical to the successful development of rockets.

Lindbergh's political views would bring him criticism during World War II. But during the war, he secretly flew combat missions in the Far East, providing the military with valuable data that helped increase the bomb-load capacity and combat radius of American aircraft.

Later in life, he would continue to serve his country, assisting in the selection of sites for the location of overseas air bases. He also became a dedicated environmentalist. His life would span the rapid development of aviation in the 20th century—Lindbergh met both the first man to fly (Orville Wright) and the first man to walk on the moon (Neil Armstrong).

The *Friendship* was a large and heavy Fokker F7 fitted with pontoons that enabled it to take off and land in water. It was painted bright colors so that it would be visible in case it crashed during its flight over the Atlantic.

Amelia. When the *Friendship* finally left Boston and headed north, after several delays due to fog, newspapers carried the triumphant message that a woman had headed into the dawn, bound for Halifax in Canada and then England. But the days of weather delay in Trepassey had dampened the enthusiasm of the media. Many hinted that the plane had failed to take off not due to the weather, but to Amelia's own fears.

The days of waiting for good weather proved stressful to Amelia and her fellow flyers. They had planned only a brief stop for refueling. They were soon forced to borrow clothing while they washed the one set of clothes they each had with them—the outfits they were wearing when they first arrived. Newspapers carried stories of other female aviators preparing to make the crossing, adding to the pressure. The crew of the *Friendship* knew that they must take off soon, or the months of preparation would have been in vain.

Day after day the crew attempted to take off, only to be forced to call off their trip because of poor weather, because the plane was too heavy to become airborne, or because the motors cut out. They plotted alternate routes—routes that would require less fuel to reach their final destination. They dumped some fuel, attempted again, and once again failed. The rain and fog continued, and so once more they were forced to wait.

On the morning of June 17 the conditions finally improved enough to permit another attempt. Only a handful of people had gathered to watch the crew of the *Friendship* make yet another effort to complete their journey. The plane was heavy with fuel tanks—the seats had been removed to install a navigation table and additional fuel supplies—and it was large, measuring nearly 72 feet (22 meters) from the tip of one wing to the other. It had been painted its distinctive bright orange color deliberately—if the plane crashed, it was hoped that the color would help rescuers locate the aircraft.

On that morning, the crew tried twice to get the heavy plane up into the air and failed both times. Finally, desperate to get the flight underway, Amelia decided upon a difficult solution—they needed to lighten the plane even more. They pumped out as much of their fuel supply as they could, leaving only the barest minimum to get them across the Atlantic. Rather than attempt to reach Southampton, England, they would leave just enough fuel to get them to Ireland—if they were lucky.

With a lightened load, the plane once more attempted to take off. The engines were soaked with saltwater spray and began to sputter, unable to produce enough power to launch the plane. The crew tried yet again. The engines continued to sputter, and the plane taxied for nearly 3 miles (5 kilometers) before suddenly, traveling at little more than 50 miles (80 kilometers) an hour, it was able to get into the air. The plane dipped, rose, and gradually wobbled its way up through the fog. It was an unimpressive beginning to what would become a historic journey.

Ships below tracked the *Friendship*'s progress as it set out across the Atlantic. Some were able to make radio contact with the plane, while others could hear its engines but not actually communicate with the crew above. The weather cleared briefly, and then, 300 miles (483 kilometers) from Trepassey, the plane was once more surrounded by clouds. The interior cabin had been stripped as part of the effort to dump anything that might weigh down the plane. Stultz and Gordon sat in the front cockpit, while Amelia was forced to sit on top of the crew's flying suits, huddled between two huge fuel tanks, since even the additional seats and cushions had been taken out to lighten their load.

The plane shook considerably, and the noise from the engines was deafening, making any kind of conversation impossible. Amelia wore earplugs to block out the noise and spent most of the flight scribbling notes in a journal, although she could see little except clouds and fog. The plane soon flew from the fog into a snow squall. There was no deicing equipment, so Stultz, who was flying at the time, was forced to quickly dive down out of the storm, sending Amelia sliding across the back of the plane.

It was a long and exhausting flight for all three crewmembers. Occasionally the fog would clear for a bit, just enough for them to catch brief glimpses of the ocean below. As the fuel was used up, the plane grew lighter and they were able to climb higher, up and out of the clouds where the visibility was better but the temperature was considerably colder. By now they were all tired and hungry—they had only a thermos of coffee to keep them awake. They put on fur-lined flying suits, scanned the skies and waited for dawn. Stultz and Gordon took turns flying, but Amelia spent most of her time crouched behind them, scribbling notes in the dark.

Finally, traces of light began to appear in the sky. The exhausted crew decided to decrease the height at which they were flying in the hope of seeing something—land, ships, anything that would help them get their bearings. They had been flying for nearly 18 hours, relying on the *Friendship*'s instruments to navigate through the poor visibility. Descending from 10,000 feet (3,048 meters) to 3,000 feet (914 meters), they could finally see the water below, but nothing else. One of their engines was making a coughing sound, and the radio did not seem to be working. Worse still, they only had two hours of fuel left.

They anxiously scanned the horizon for signs of land. Finally, they spotted several ships in the water below. But the ships were cutting across their course, not sailing parallel to it, as they should have been if the *Friendship* was flying toward land. Confused, the crew attempted to make contact with the ships, but the radio was still not working. Finally, Stultz used up some of their precious fuel supply to backtrack and circle above one of the boats. Amelia scribbled a hasty note asking for their position, attached it to an orange, and attempted to throw it down onto the deck of the ocean liner. She missed. The ship sailed on. And the *Friendship* had only one hour of fuel left.

For 30 minutes they flew on through the mist, uncertain of where they were or whether they were headed in the right direction. Finally, they saw a fishing boat below, then several more. And then, at last, a shadow appeared on the horizon that, as they approached, proved to be land. Even though they did not know where they were, but they were very happy to be there.

FLIGHT TO FAME

On a misty, rainy morning on June 18, 1928, a plane appeared out of the clouds and landed in the ocean outside the small town of Burry Port in South Wales. The people nearby paid little attention to the plane or its crew as they went about their daily activities. Longshoremen loading coal nearby responded to the waves of the crew with friendly waves of their own, boats passed by with cheerful cries of "ship ahoy!" but even the news that the plane and its crew had flown across the Atlantic caused little excitement.

Finally, after about an hour of exchanging waves, a boat rowed out to the exhausted flyers and they were escorted to shore. Approximately 20 hours and 49 minutes after departure, Amelia Earhart had become the first woman to fly across the Atlantic.

The subdued reception in the small Welsh village was due in part to the fact that the flyers had been expected in Southampton, England, where a huge reception had been arranged. But as reporters learned of the *Friendship*'s arrival, and word of the "girl pilot" spread, a crowd soon gathered to cheer this historic event. The crew was quickly escorted to a hotel, where hot baths and the first group of interviewers awaited. Stultz and Gordon were essentially ignored. It was Amelia that the reporters had come to interview. The woman who described herself as "just a passenger," who claimed to have contributed little more to the historic voyage than a "sack of potatoes," had become a celebrity.

Telegrams poured in congratulating Amelia, including one from U.S. President Calvin Coolidge. The crew finally took off for their destination of Southampton the next day, and this time Amelia earned her media label of "girl pilot" by spending part of the flight at the controls. A much more elaborate celebration greeted their arrival this time. They were escorted by an Imperial Airways Sea Eagle, an amphibian biplane billed as the first passenger flying boat service. Crowds cheered, tugboats blew their whistles, and foghorns blasted. The crew enjoyed a whirlwind round of press conferences (focusing almost exclusively on Amelia). Then they went on to London, where Amelia was wined and dined by some of England's leading socialites and political figures. Some 32 American cities issued invitations, wanting to host parades in the flyers' honor when they returned to the United States.

The flight across the Atlantic had transformed the shy 30-year-old American social worker into an international figure. A journey of less than 21 hours had earned her a place in aviation history, but it was not the first of her astonishing accomplishments—and it would not be the last.

Earhart (front, left) and pilot Bill Stultz were congratulated by the mayor of Southampton and his wife. The crew had finally arrived in Southampton after landing first in Burry Port, South Wales.

The Feeling
of Flying

Even as a little girl, Amelia Earhart loved the sensation of soaring through the air. When she was seven years old, she designed a roller coaster and, with the help of her younger sister, Muriel, began to build it in her family's yard. For days, while the other little girls in their Kansas neighborhood did the things nice little girls were expected to do in 1904—playing house, sewing doll's clothes— Amelia and her sister hammered and sawed a stack of wooden boards and old fence rails to construct their roller coaster.

The finished track began at the ridgepole on the top of the shed. Amelia and her sister had built a small car from a 9-by-12-inch (23-by-30-centimeter) wooden board with roller-skate wheels attached to its bottom. Little blonde-haired Amelia was the first to test the ride, racing down the handmade shoot at a high rate of speed before hitting the ground below. Part of the wooden coaster splintered and the wheels gave out a loud squeal.

16

The first trip down was an experiment. Amelia quickly decided that the end of the ride needed to be fixed—it needed more track, and the wood at the end of the chute that had splintered would need to be replaced. After these adjustments had been made, Amelia went down again, this time calling out with joy at the sensation of flying through the air.

Years later, George Putnam, Amelia's husband, would explain that the story of the roller coaster showed how Amelia would

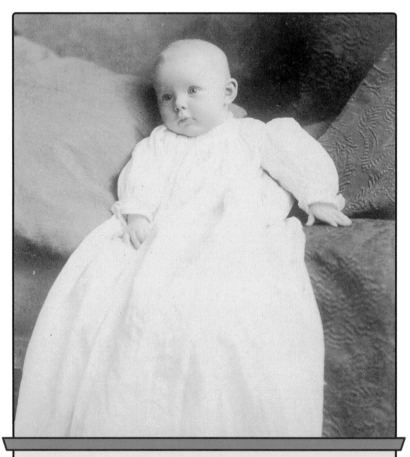

Amelia's family encouraged adventure, physical fitness, and experimentation. She was the first-born daughter of Amy Otis—a wealthy, forward-thinking woman—and a lawyer named Edwin Earhart.

George Putnam

The man who jokingly referred to himself as "Mr. Earhart" after his marriage to the world's most famous female aviator was much more than a successful promoter of his wife's career, although his genius for publicity undoubtedly contributed to her fame.

George Palmer Putnam was born on September 7, 1887, to a publishing family. He grew up surrounded by books, but as his older brother was the one destined to enter the family business, George decided to find adventure in the West. He moved to the frontier town of Bend, Oregon, in 1909, where at the age of 21 he became the town's publicity officer. Less than a year later, he owned the local newspaper, the *Bulletin*, and became its editor. He married his first wife, Dorothy Binney, the daughter of a wealthy industrialist. At the age of 24 he was elected Bend's mayor.

George enjoyed a successful career in the west. He wrote books about his adventures, then was chosen to move to Salem, Oregon, to serve as a private secretary to the governor. When World War I broke out, George (a member of the National Guard) was ordered into service in Mexico, where he spent most of his time filing dispatches for the *Bulletin*.

George's older brother died in 1918, and so when he was discharged from the army, he returned to New York where he began work at G.P. Putnam's Sons. George became a brilliant publisher, creating the concept of "fabricated books"—developing an idea for a book and then finding the author to write it. He published a number of notable authors, including Ben Hecht and Dorothy Parker, and he included among his friends Charlie Chaplin, Franklin Roosevelt, and Admiral Richard Byrd.

He was inspired by the adventure books he published to make his own expeditions, including one to the Arctic. His success publishing *We*, Charles Lindbergh's memoir of his historic flight, would prompt George to become interested when he learned that another "first" flight across the Atlantic would be attempted, this one with a woman on board.

After his marriage to Amelia, George continued to work as a publisher in New York, and then later in the film business in Hollywood. After Amelia's death, George arranged for the posthumous publication of her memoir, titled *Last Flight*, and wrote several books of his own. He influenced and inspired countless writers, sharing his business skills and enthusiasm and helping to shape the careers of many talented people.

come to approach the experience of real flight—in an airplane. Her adventurous spirit would not be contained by what was expected of girls, or women. Accidents and mishaps would not stop her or force her to give up. Instead, she would try again and again until she had succeeded in whatever she was attempting.

KANSAS GIRL

While Amelia's mother eventually insisted that the dangerous roller coaster be taken apart, there were other adventures that marked Amelia's early years. She was born on July 24, 1897, at the luxurious home of her mother's parents in Atchison, Kansas. She was named Amelia Mary Earhart, Amelia and Mary being the names of her two grandmothers.

Her mother's family—Judge and Mrs. Alfred Otis—was one of the wealthiest and most influential families in the town of Atchison, and Amelia spent much of her childhood at their home. Amelia's mother, Amy, had grown up in a wealthy family but had not led a sheltered life. Her father had been one of the earliest settlers of that part of Kansas and encouraged his children to see and learn about as much of America as they could. They traveled throughout Colorado, Oklahoma, and Utah, seeing parts of America before it had been settled. Amy would become the first woman to climb Pikes Peak in Colorado during a trip with her father in the summer of 1890. It was not an easy climb—for 10,000 feet (3,048 meters) they rode on donkeys, but the remainder of the climb was made on foot. Many men in the party suffered from nosebleeds because of the height and decided to turn back, but 21-year-old Amy managed the dangerous final quarter-mile and reached the top.

That same summer, Amy met a young lawyer named Edwin Stanton Earhart. His family was far less wealthy than Amy's. Edwin was the son of a Lutheran minister from western Pennsylvania who had moved his family to Kansas in 1856, the same year that Edwin (the youngest of 12 children) was born. To help pay for his college education, Edwin built furnaces, shined shoes, cared for horses, and tutored other students.

Amy's father, Judge Otis, had higher ambitions for his daughter than marriage to a poor country lawyer. When Edwin asked for permission to marry Amy, her father granted it—on one condition. Edwin must prove that he could earn at least $50 a month for six months in a row. It took Edwin five years before he could offer the necessary proof that he could support the judge's daughter and the couple could be married. They moved to Kansas City, where Amy's parents presented them with a fully furnished house as a wedding present.

Two and a half years after Amelia's birth, her sister Muriel was born. The sisters were very close and were encouraged to explore and be adventurous, particularly by their mother. While most little girls were taught to move slowly and sedately, confined by their long skirts, Amelia's mother allowed her daughters to dress in dark-blue flannel suits with bloomers, which allowed them to run and play freely. These outfits would seem old-fashioned and very conservative today, but in the early part of the 20th century they were considered almost revolutionary.

Amy encouraged her daughters' curiosity. She allowed them to stay up late to see the eclipse of the moon, and in 1908 the entire family climbed up on the roof of their shed to watch Halley's comet. The girls and their mother took nature walks and collected worms, moths, spiders, and toads to bring home. When a chicken was slaughtered for dinner, their mother had the girls watch, pointing out the different parts of the chicken's body and showing them how the lungs and heart worked. The girls were allowed to sled down hills in the winter, not on the high sleds with wooden runners that little girls in the neighborhood sat properly in, but instead on low sleds with steel runners that the girls would run beside and then jump on, whooping down the icy hill on their stomachs at top speed.

It was a childhood that taught Amelia a love for speed, a desire for adventure, and a willingness to try new things—

This family portrait of the Earharts was taken in Atchison, Kansas, where they lived until 1908. Amelia is the young girl in the white dress at the center of this photograph.

things that other girls would not do. Amelia rode horses—there were still only a few cars in Kansas—and spent a lot of time at her grandparents' home reading and playing. The girls enjoyed a privileged life until 1908, when they moved with their parents to Des Moines, Iowa, where Edwin had been offered a new job in the claims department of a railroad.

It was a move that would mean a radical change in 11-year-old Amelia's life. The family home had no park, barn, or orchard to play in. She was far from her cousins, with whom she had always played, and could no longer attend the private school she had enjoyed in Kansas. Just before Amelia and

Muriel were set to enroll in the local public school in their new home, their mother was informed that their hair should be cut, as it was likely that they might contract lice in the classroom. The plans to attend the local school were canceled, and instead a private tutor was hired for a few months before the cost made it necessary for the girls to venture into the public school.

It was also in 1908 that Amelia would see her first airplane, at the Iowa State Fair. The Wright brothers had made their first flight five years earlier, and public interest in airplanes was high. But Amelia was far more interested in a paper hat shaped like a peach basket than in the invention that would make her famous.

A BROKEN FAMILY

There were some happy times in the early years after the family moved to Des Moines. Amelia's father traveled through-out the country for his work and often took his family with him as he crossed the United States in a private railroad car. They all spent summers at a lake in Minnesota, where Amelia went horseback riding, and spent time fishing and playing tennis. But by 1910, the happy times were becoming fewer. Her father had developed a drinking problem, and his alcoholism ultimately cost him his job.

The family was forced to move to St. Paul, Minnesota, where Amelia's father found a new job at a much lower salary. Her father's income barely provided enough money for the family. In winter, they could not afford to heat their whole house, so the family spent those cold months together in the two rooms they could keep heated. In September 1911, Amelia's Grandmother Otis died (her grandfather had died a few years earlier), and the home where Amelia had spent so many happy years as a girl was sold. Mrs. Otis was aware of her son-in-law's alcoholism, and so her will dictated that the portion of her substantial estate that was to go to Amy, Amelia's mother, was to be put into trust for 20 years or until Edwin had died.

It was a clear indication of the disgust his in-laws held for him, and it prompted Edwin to drink even more heavily. Once more he lost his job; once more the family moved, although this time in separate directions. Amelia's father headed for Kansas City, where he lived with his sister. Amelia, Amy, and Muriel moved to Chicago.

Amelia excelled in science and math at her new school—Hyde Park High School—but she had few friends and was described in her class picture as "the girl in brown, who walks alone." It was a difficult time for Amelia; her father's illness had shattered the family. She had attended six different high schools in four years. The family had gone from their elite status as members of the respected Judge Otis family to members of a broken family living in a cheap apartment. Amelia began to look toward graduating from high school and making plans to attend college.

Amelia's family briefly came back together in Kansas City after she had graduated from high school. Her father persuaded her mother to contest the Otis will, and ultimately a settlement was reached that provided enough money for Amelia and her sister to attend private schools that would prepare them for college. Amelia enrolled at the Ogontz School in Philadelphia, hoping that the prep school would help her reach her ultimate goal—attending Bryn Mawr College.

LEARNING AND LEADERSHIP

When she was 19 years old, Amelia left her family and headed for boarding school. The Ogontz School was exclusive and conservative; the students came principally from wealthy families and much of their time was devoted to studying fine arts, listening to lectures given by famous writers, and attending concerts and the opera in nearby Philadelphia. Amelia played hockey and basketball, read extensively, and led a protest against the cliques that divided the school into secret sororities.

Her letters home during this time reveal an awareness of events outside the sheltered walls of her boarding school. World War I had broken out, and Amelia soon volunteered for the American Red Cross. For Christmas 1917, Amelia went to Toronto, Canada, where her younger sister was attending boarding school. Her mother joined the girls there for the holiday.

In Toronto, Amelia saw the first clear signs of the tragedy of war. Wounded soldiers back from the front were everywhere, and the sight of men missing arms and legs, blinded, or paralyzed, deeply affected her.

Amelia returned to Ogontz after the holiday but the sheltered environment of the school felt oppressive and meaningless. By February 1918, her mother had given Amelia permission to leave the school without completing her senior year. She quickly returned to Toronto, where she spent time working as a nurses' aide at the Spadina Military Hospital.

The nursing work was challenging and difficult. Amelia was responsible for caring for patients from 7 A.M. to 7 P.M., with a break of only two hours in the afternoon. She was responsible for washing patients' trays and even scrubbing the hospital floors. She spent time serving meals and spooning out medicine from buckets. Seeing up close the devastating effects of war, she became a firm pacifist, and the distaste for war would stay with her for the rest of her life.

Among the patients she cared for were several French and British pilots. One of them, a captain with the Royal Flying Corps, invited Amelia and her sister Muriel to an exhibition of stunt flying. Something about the excitement and drama of the small red plane, soaring overhead in nearly impossible twists and dives, appealed to her. She spent much of her free time at the airfield, watching the pilots train.

A serious flu epidemic swept through the hospital in the fall of 1918. Amelia worked night and day, caring for the patients and staff members who had fallen ill. She too would ultimately become sick, and when the armistice was signed on

During World War I, Amelia worked as an aide in a hospital in Toronto, Canada. Her experiences with wounded soldiers led to her lifelong distaste for war. She spent some of her free time during this period watching exhibitions at local airfields.

November 11, 1918, signaling the end of World War I, Amelia soon traveled to Northampton, Massachusetts, to stay with her sister while she recovered.

She rested for several months, recovering from her illness and worrying about what to do with the rest of her life. Her sister enrolled at Smith College, and Amelia soon signed up for an automobile engine repair class at the college. She became quite skillful at repairing motors—a talent that would prove helpful with vehicles in the air as well as on the ground.

Amelia had been inspired by her nursing work and finally decided to study medicine. She enrolled in Columbia University in the fall of 1919 as a premed student. She was 22 years old. She soon discovered that practicing medicine was of little interest, but continued in her studies, thinking that perhaps she might pursue a career in medical research.

Meanwhile, Amelia's father was now living in California and desperate to have his family rejoin him. Amelia's mother finally agreed to leave Massachusetts, where she had been living near Muriel, if Amelia would also agree to return west with her. At the age of 23, Amelia left New York and headed for her parents' new home in Los Angeles. She was still struggling to determine how she would spend her life, but her short-term goal was clear: She would do her best to keep her parents together until her younger sister graduated from college. Then she would return to New York and live her own life.

In Los Angeles, Amelia soon began spending time at the several airfields near her home, just as she had done in Toronto. One Sunday, she went with her father to an air show at Daugherty Field in Long Beach. She saw a pilot and asked her father to find out the cost of flying lessons. The answer: $1,000.

The sum was well beyond what they could afford, but Amelia's father decided to arrange for Amelia to go up in an airplane for a quick ride the following day, perhaps thinking that the trip would be enough to wipe out his daughter's interest in spending more time in the sky. The next morning, they went to Rogers Field, a small strip of dirt near Wilshire Boulevard, where for $10 Amelia was given a 10-minute ride. The pilot was a young man named Frank Hawks, who would go on to break many speed records in the air.

The plane soared up over the Hollywood hills. The ocean

was visible in the distance. It was a moment that would change Amelia's life. At 200 feet (61 meters) up in the air, Amelia knew that flying was what she was meant to do.

LEARNING TO FLY

Amelia returned from the airfield determined to learn how to fly. Her father made it clear that he could not afford the expensive lessons, so Amelia decided to earn the money herself. She found an office job with the Los Angeles Telephone Company, and soon she was spending weekdays at work and weekends at the primitive Long Beach airport known as Kinner Field.

Her first instructor was a woman pilot named Anita (Neta) Snook. It was 1920, and there were few women pilots and even fewer female flight instructors. Snook was the first woman to graduate from the Curtiss School of Aviation. She was only a year older than Amelia but had been flying ever since she left school. She had attempted to enter the U.S. Air Force, but had been turned down because she was a woman. So she had moved to Canada, where she worked for the British war effort inspecting airplane engines being assembled there.

After World War I, Snook bought a damaged Canadian training plane, rebuilt it, and then flew her way across the country, taking up paying passengers for 15-minute flights, doing aerial advertising, performing stunts, and teaching people how to fly. She would later remember her first sight of Amelia, coming across the field with her father, as a tall, slender young woman, accompanied by an elderly man who was neat and well dressed. Amelia asked to be taught how to fly and agreed to pay for her lessons each day at a rate of one dollar per minute.

On January 3, 1921, Amelia arrived for her first flying lesson. She was wearing old brown riding breeches, a brown jacket, and boots. She spent her first 30 minutes learning how to taxi the plane—the old Curtiss Canuck biplane that Snook used for

Edwin Stanton Earhart was not in the position to support his daughter's growing interest in becoming a pilot. He was plagued with health and financial problems, and his marriage to Amy, which had been troubled for years, was ending.

training would-be pilots. Amelia spent the first weeks on the ground, learning how to operate the plane, working the controls, and studying the basic principles of flight, as well as listening to the pilots in the hangar and asking questions about flying.

Amelia was determined to learn all that she could. Her

weekends were a blur of reading about flying, learning how to work the plane, and then hanging around the pilots at the airfield. It was not an easy commute. To get to the airport, Amelia traveled for more than an hour by streetcar, then walked several miles to reach the airport. She soon cut her hair short, copying the style of Snook and the other pilots. After about six months' of lessons, she settled on a new goal: She wanted to buy her own airplane.

And she had found what she thought was the perfect plane—a small biplane known as the "Kinner Airster." It was a lightweight two-seater powered by a three-cylinder engine. It would travel for 500 miles (805 kilometers) at speeds up to 85 miles per hour (137 kilometers per hour).

When Amelia shared her dream with her teacher, Neta Snook was concerned. She felt that the Kinner had an unreliable engine and was too sophisticated a plane for a beginning pilot, less stable than the Canuck that Amelia was learning how to fly.

But Amelia was determined, and in July 1921, Amelia bought her first airplane for a price of $2,000. The plane was bright yellow, and she named it the *Canary.* Amelia borrowed money from her mother and sister and used up all of her own savings for the plane. She had nothing left to pay for her lessons, but Snook agreed to teach her how to operate the Kinner for free. Amelia had no money, she was not yet ready to fly on her own, but she had her own airplane.

A New Career

A melia now had a new-found purpose: She worked to fly. Her paychecks were quickly spent on the loans for her plane, on lessons, on fuel, and on a new leather flying coat. She took several part-time jobs to pay for flying, working at the telephone company, as a photographer's assistant, and for her father.

In fact, financial difficulties were affecting her entire family. The family decided to rent rooms to boarders. One of them was a young chemical engineer named Sam Chapman, who soon began dating Amelia. Amelia enjoyed spending time with Sam, but her focus remained on flying.

And her flying was beginning to bring her attention. She was interviewed in the Los Angeles *Examiner* in 1922, describing her plan to fly her plane across the country the following year. She also made her first attempt to break a record. In October, Amelia invited her father and sister to an exhibition at Rogers Field. Once she gave them their tickets, she disappeared. Only a short while later, they saw her taking off. When she returned about an hour later, they learned—from loudspeakers broadcasting to the field—that she had just broken the women's altitude record, flying her plane to 14,000 feet (4,267 meters). The record stood for only a few weeks before being broken by another female pilot—Ruth Nichols—but it would prove to be the first in a lifetime of challenges and achievements for Amelia.

This Kinner Airster was the first plane that Amelia purchased. She had to work several jobs to pay for the bright yellow plane, which she called the *Canary*, and its maintenance.

Not all of her attempts were successful. Flying was unreliable in those early days of aviation. The planes were slow; the engines could suddenly begin to sputter or give out. Amelia had several close calls, where her plane went into a spin or the plane turned over on landing, but she persisted in her desire to fly—and to excel at flying.

On May 16, 1923, Amelia was granted a certificate officially labeling her as an "Aviator Pilot" from the Fédération Aeronautique Internationale. In those days, it was not necessary to have this type of license to fly, but it was required to make attempts on official records.

In 1923 the family finances reached a critical point. Amelia had persuaded her parents to invest in a small mining business owned by a friend of hers. The business failed, and much of her mother's inheritance was lost. To help pay back some of the money, Amelia decided to sell her Kinner airplane. Her father's health was poor, and her parents' marriage, after several difficult years, was finally coming to an end. In 1924 they divorced, and Amelia, her mother, and sister decided to move to the East Coast, to Massachusetts. Amelia had hoped to fly across the country, but this plan was abandoned and, rather than make the trip by train, Amelia decided to buy another yellow vehicle, this one a car. It was a convertible, with wire wheels and two steps on either side to get in and out, and it soon became known as the "Yellow Peril."

Muriel, Amelia's sister, went by train to Boston, where she was attending classes at Harvard. Amelia and her mother decided to take the scenic route back across the country, and so they drove north to Yosemite, then Seattle, then on to Lake Louise and Banff in Canada. It was still quite unusual to travel across the country by automobile. They traveled along simple, two-lane roads—there were no highways then—attracting attention in a bright yellow car that was soon covered in tourist stickers.

But at the end of the journey, Amelia found that she once more was uncertain what to do with her time. She enrolled briefly at Columbia University in New York, but spent only a few months there before rejoining her mother and sister in Boston. She was 27 years old, but still uncertain how she would spend the rest of her life.

SOCIAL WORKER

In the fall of 1925, Amelia took a job as a social worker at Denison House in Boston. She had no experience in the field, but her new employer, Marion Perkins, was impressed by Amelia's manner and speech, as well as by the fact that she held a pilot's license. It soon became clear that Amelia had a real talent for the work—teaching English to poor immigrant men and women. She learned about their native cultures and languages while teaching them the best ways to handle life in Boston. She gave some of the children their first ride in an automobile—her own Yellow Peril—and drove others to the hospital or for citizenship tests.

Amelia reconnected with other pilots as well. She joined the Boston chapter of the National Aeronautic Association, ultimately becoming its vice president. She spent much of her free time on weekends at the airfield. Once more, the papers began to publish pictures of Amelia, either near or inside a plane.

By 1927, Amelia had become a full-time staff member at Denison House, as well as serving as secretary to its board of directors. Just as her career as a social worker was taking off, another flyer made history. Charles Lindbergh became the first person to make a successful transatlantic flight—crossing the Atlantic Ocean alone. His flight would transform aviation and would transform Amelia's life, too. A bit less than a year after Lindbergh crossed the Atlantic Ocean, Amelia was called to the telephone as she was helping to organize a class play. On the

Charles Lindbergh, or "Lucky Lindy," made the first nonstop solo flight across the Atlantic Ocean in 1927. His accomplishments inspired a generation of men and women in the field of aviation.

phone was a man named Captain Hilton H. Railey. He wanted to know if Amelia was interested in becoming the first woman to fly across the Atlantic Ocean.

AN UNUSUAL INTERVIEW

Amelia was invited to New York to meet with attorney David T. Layman and John Phipps, the brother of the wealthy Mrs. Amy Guest, who would be the financial backer of the flight. Also at the meeting was publisher George Palmer Putnam, whose company—G.P. Putnam's Sons—had enjoyed spectacular success by publishing Charles Lindbergh's *We*, a memoir of his historic flight across the Atlantic. Putnam had learned that another transatlantic attempt was going to be made, and this time it would include a woman. He was eager to sign her up so that, in the event that the trip would succeed, he could publish yet another transatlantic memoir, this one by a female author.

Amy Guest had hoped to make the flight herself, but her family persuaded her that it would be too dangerous. She was quite specific about the kind of woman that she wanted on the flight—one who was attractive, well educated, and had the kind of good manners that would make her acceptable to the English society where she would be welcomed upon her arrival on the other side of the Atlantic.

There were several female pilots who were being considered, including Ruth Nichols and Ruth Elder. But Amelia's appearance gave her a distinct advantage. With her boyish figure, short hair, and blue eyes, she bore a startling resemblance to Lindbergh, and the publicity angle for this "Lady Lindy" became clear to all those involved in the project.

Amelia was very interested in making the flight and instinctively understood how best to conduct herself during the interview. She would later remember that the secret was in getting those involved to like her enough to want to work with her, but not like her so much that they would not want to send her out on a dangerous expedition. Her goal, she recalled, was to be completely mediocre.

It seems unlikely that she was chosen because she was "mediocre." In fact, Putnam was impressed enough to immediately decide that she would be the woman to make the flight. Two days after the meeting, Amelia was officially informed that she had been chosen to make the dangerous trip—without any pay. It was an offer she could not refuse.

FRIENDSHIP

Amelia's flight across the Atlantic on board the *Friendship* would bring her great fame. It would also mark the beginning of her lifelong partnership with Putnam, first as her supporter and admirer, later as her publisher, and still later as her husband.

Because the plans to make the transatlantic flight had to be guarded with great secrecy, Amelia could only take occasional glimpses of the plane before her actual flight. In fact, she saw it only twice before the departure from Boston. It was the largest airplane in which Amelia had ever flown. Its bright colors—red-orange with gold wings—made it stand out on the Boston airfield, and since Amelia was fairly well known in Boston aviation circles, she was told to stay away from the plane to avoid any speculation that she might be making an attempt to become the first woman to cross the Atlantic.

As the plane was made ready for the voyage, Amelia spent time with Putnam, ultimately entrusting him with the letters for her family that were to be given out should she not return from the trip. His telegrams encouraged her while the crew was stranded in Newfoundland, and his extraordinary publicity skills were put into practice as soon as the flight was underway.

Upon her return, George ensured that Amelia was constantly

in the public eye. He arranged hundreds of speaking engagements. Magazines and newspapers were eager to publish her written stories about her flight. It soon became clear that Amelia's career as a social worker had ended when she took her leave of absence from Denison House to prepare for the flight. She was now a famous aviator.

Because interest in her story was so high, Amelia quickly began work on the book that would record her experiences flying across the ocean. The book needed to be prepared in weeks, to ensure that it was published before interest in her story began to fade. By early September 1928, the book—to be titled *20 Hrs. 40 Min.* after the amount of time it took to make the crossing—had been finished, and Amelia began to look around for new opportunities.

She and George Putnam both had a strong interest in ensuring that Amelia continued to remain in the public eye. Amelia wanted to be able to make a living—a good living—for herself by flying; Putnam wanted to continue to publicize Amelia's flying to ensure strong sales for her book.

While in England, Amelia had met a new friend, Lady Mary Heath, who was also a skilled pilot. Lady Heath had flown solo from South Africa to England and had allowed Amelia to make a quick flight in the famous Avian Moth in which she had made her own record-breaking flight. Amelia had loved the feel of the plane and offered to buy it from Lady Heath and have it shipped back to America. Shortly after Amelia had finished writing her book, the Avian arrived from England, and Amelia decided to take a vacation, flying from the East Coast back to Los Angeles. News of the trip (no doubt sparked by Putnam) attracted reporters. Amelia carefully plotted out each stop on her trip west. It was not an easy journey. Many of the airfields that existed across the country bore little resemblance to the smooth runways in use today. They were simple strips of grass or dirt, unmarked and difficult to spot from above. The towns and cities all looked the same from the air, and Amelia was forced to rely on maps and educated guesses, in one stop landing on the main street of a small town when she could not find the airfield. When she finally arrived in Los Angeles, it was as the holder of another record—the first woman to fly solo from the East Coast to the West Coast.

She visited with her father for a few days and then decided to fly back to New York. She encountered engine trouble on an early part of the journey and was forced to make a quick landing in Utah, where the plane was damaged. After the plane was finally repaired, Amelia set out once more, landing in New York on October 16 and earning yet another "first"—the first woman to fly solo across the continent and back.

SPEAKER AND ROLE MODEL

Amelia returned to New York to begin the lecture tour that Putnam had arranged. The schedule was hectic and exhausting, requiring her to make as many as 30 speeches per month in 27 different cities—at colleges and universities and before a variety of men's and women's groups. She became a skilled speaker—she was enthusiastic about flight, and her love of the subject came across to her audience.

In the scarce downtime she had, traveling from one city to the next, she was busy writing articles. She had been given a contract by *Cosmopolitan* magazine to write eight articles per year, as well as respond to letters and questions from readers. Amelia shared her thoughts on pilot training, on whether or not girls should be allowed to learn how to fly, on air safety, and on the facilities various airports offered. She soon took on a larger role in encouraging women to fly with her appointment as assistant to the general traffic manager of Transcontinental Air Transport (TAT), one of the earliest attempts at a national airline. TAT would later

Amelia is shown wearing the standard attire of pilots at that time, including goggles and a leather hat and coat. Maps and airfields during the early days of aviation were poorly marked, and tested the talents of pilots.

grow into Trans World Airlines (TWA), but in those early years TAT gave appointments to famous aviators like Earhart and Lindbergh (who served as chairman of its technical committee) to help project a public image of aviation.

TAT hoped to reassure women about aviation safety, prompting them to feel safer about their husbands using airplanes for business travel and, perhaps, to consider flying themselves. The goal was to transform aviation from its reputation as a dangerous sport to an alternative for commercial transportation. Amelia took on the assignment of persuading women about the safety of aviation, frequently taking her mother with her on short flights for TAT.

Amelia had also joined forces with several other female pilots to create an organization for women pilots as well as to launch a cross-country air race for women only. This Women's Air Derby was scheduled to mark the opening of the National Air Races. The flyers set out on August 18, 1929, from Clover Field in Santa Monica, California, heading for Cleveland, Ohio. The race was scheduled to last for eight days, and 20 women pilots were participating. The prize for the pilot who won: $2,500.

There was no system of classification to distinguish between pilots flying bigger, heavier planes and those flying smaller aircraft. Clearly, a pilot operating a larger, more powerful plane stood a better chance of winning. Amelia's small Avian would be no match for some of the larger aircraft competing, so shortly before the race began Amelia sold the Avian and purchased a new plane, a more powerful Lockheed Vega. The Vega was one of the fastest airplanes then available, but it was also much more difficult to operate. The cockpit was much higher off the ground than previous planes Amelia had flown, and its fuselage was much weaker, prone to quick collapse in a forced landing.

Among the famous female pilots participating in the race were Ruth Nichols, Louise Thaden, and Blanche Noyes, all of whom at one point had hoped to become the first woman to fly across the Atlantic. The first leg of the race was a short trip of approximately 60 miles (97 kilometers) to the east, to San Bernardino. The first day passed without incident, but the rest of the race was a test of both endurance and skill. Amelia damaged her plane's propeller in Arizona. Marvel Crosson's airplane crashed in Phoenix, and she was killed. Two other pilots were forced to land when sand was discovered in their fuel tank. In fact there were several forced landings during the course of the race. Pilots would land their planes, repair or adjust as needed, and then take off again.

The courage and skill demonstrated by the women pilots was remarkable. The conditions in those early years of flying made the race all the more challenging. The only navigation tool most pilots had was a compass. There were few aviation maps—most pilots had to rely on road maps. They often landed without being absolutely certain of where they were. One pilot was forced to make a landing in a field of cattle; another took off suffering from what she thought was the flu, only to later be forced to abandon the race because she was stricken with typhoid fever. Pilot Blanche Noyes, flying 3,000 feet (914 meters) above Texas, realized that her plane was on fire. She landed, threw sand on the plane to extinguish the flames, and then took off again.

When the race finally ended, 16 women crossed the finish line. It was the highest percentage of people (men or women) to ever finish a cross-country race. Louise Thaden was the winner, Gladys O'Donnell crossed the finish line just a brief time later, and Amelia arrived third. Despite having what was probably the most powerful plane in the race, Amelia crossed the finish line nearly two hours after the winner.

The race was an important achievement for all women interested in aviation, and only a few days later Amelia and a group of the other competitors (including O'Donnell, Thaden, and Nichols) met to sketch out their idea for an organization for women pilots. Their aim was to unite women pilots and create a forum for activities that would benefit women aviators and aviation in general. There were 117 women holding piloting licenses at the time that the organization was being formed, and all of them were invited to join. In the end, 99 women pilots responded, and the group became known as the Ninety-Nines. Amelia would be elected its first president in March 1931.

The Ninety-Nines

On October 9, 1929, a letter was sent out to the 117 licensed female pilots in the United States, inviting them to become part of a new organization. Signed by four well-known pilots—Fay Gillis, Margorie Brown, Frances Harrell, and Neva Paris—the letter promised an opportunity for the aviators to get acquainted and discuss prospects for women pilots from both a "sports and breadwinning point of view." On November 2, 1929, 26 female aviators gathered at Curtiss Field on Long Island, New York, to make plans for this new organization of licensed women pilots.

Several different names for the group were discussed, among them Climbing Vines, Bird Women, Gad Flies, Angel's Club, and Skylarks. But it was Amelia Earhart, who would go on to become the group's first president, who came up with the name that would stick. She proposed naming it for the total number of charter members. When 99 women finally agreed to join the fledgling group, it was named the "Ninety-Nines."

The group's original goal was to coordinate the efforts of women in aviation, to assist them with aeronautical research, air racing, and even in acquiring aerial experience. It became an important force in aviation, providing female pilots with support and new opportunities.

Today, the Ninety-Nines is an international organization, with more than 6,500 members from 35 different countries.

The Ninety-Nines was a group of women pilots who joined together to provide resources for women as they carved out their place in early aviation. Amelia was the organization's first president.

A NEW LOVE

Amelia was enjoying a period of strong professional achievement as the 1920s came to an end. She was proud of her role as president of the Ninety-Nines, proud of the records she had broken and proud of what she had achieved as a role model. Personally, her life was changing, too. The relationship with George Putnam that had begun as a professional one had gradually transformed into something more personal, as the admiration each felt for the other grew. Putnam was greatly responsible for successfully promoting Amelia as the "world's greatest female pilot," even though other women aviators had made noteworthy, and perhaps even more impressive, flights. They had spent long periods of time together, shaping her career at its earliest stages and then celebrating its success together.

Putnam proposed twice before Amelia finally agreed to become his wife. She was concerned that marriage would mean an end to her freedom, and she repeatedly stressed, both to Putnam and others, that she could not become the kind of wife that would be content to stay at home, keeping house and caring for her husband. The unhappiness of her parents' marriage had deeply affected her.

In the end, she agreed to become Mrs. George Putnam. On a cold Saturday, February 7, 1931, the couple was married at the home of Putnam's mother in Noank, Connecticut. It was a small and simple ceremony, arranged hastily at the last minute by George's mother when, two days earlier, her son phoned and told her that they would be arriving the very next day to be married. The only guests were two witnesses and George's mother. A judge who was a friend of the family performed the ceremony. Amelia wore a simple brown suit with brown shoes.

Just before the ceremony began, Amelia handed Putnam a letter, carefully written in pencil with a few words crossed out. It was a letter outlining her fears about marriage, her worries that their partnership might somehow be changed by the wedding, and her concerns that she would no longer be able to pursue her career with the kind of focus that she had before. She stressed that she would consider them both free, not bound to each other in some old-fashioned way but instead able to continue with their work as they both chose. It was an astonishingly modern view of marriage.

"I may have to keep some place where I can go to be myself now and then," she wrote. In the end, she requested that Putnam agree to promise that he would let her go in a year if she was unhappy in the marriage.

Putnam agreed to her terms, and they were married, borrowing a ring from the groom's mother, as they had not had time to buy their own. The couple spent an hour or so chatting after the wedding and then headed off for a very quick celebration. They were both so busy that there was no time for a honeymoon. Marriage was an important step, but not one that would be allowed to interfere with Amelia's career.

Solo Across the Atlantic

Amelia was very busy and focused on her career in the months following her marriage. Her father had died shortly before her wedding to Putnam, and she had been increasingly assuming financial responsibility for her mother and her sister, who was struggling with an unhappy marriage. Amelia searched for new ways to further her career and to expand her skills and her reputation.

There were fewer and fewer "firsts" available. Many of the top records and challenges had already been seized by top women pilots. Finally, Amelia decided to test her skills with a new kind of vehicle, known as an autogiro. The autogiro was a kind of hybrid aircraft, a combination of an airplane and a helicopter. It was a relatively new vehicle, and no other woman was flying one.

First, Amelia set altitude records in the autogiro, reaching nearly 19,000 feet (5,791 meters) on April 8, 1931. Because her attempt in the autogiro brought some good publicity, she decided to try to break additional records, first purchasing her own Pitcairn autogiro in May of the same year. The autogiro was then resold to the Beech-Nut Company, a manufacturer of chewing gum. In a deal arranged by Putnam, Beech-Nut agreed to loan the plane to Amelia and pay her a fee for flying it for them, winning

Amelia was always in search of new ways to demonstrate her prowess in the air. This search sometimes cost her dearly—in 1931, she survived a crash while flying stunts in a Detroit air show.

publicity for herself and the company at the same time.

As part of the publicity campaign, Amelia decided to become the first person to fly coast to coast in an autogiro. She set out on May 39, 1931, from Newark, New Jersey, heading for the West Coast. Dozens of stops were arranged along the way, in which packets of Beech-Nut chewing gum were given away to the crowds gathered to cheer on Amelia. She finally landed in Los Angeles on June 7, only to be given the disappointing news that someone else—a young pilot named Johnny Miller—had flown coast-to-coast in an autogiro only a week earlier.

Amelia decided that if she could not be the first person to go from the East Coast to the West Coast in an autogiro, she would become the first person to make the reverse trip. She immediately decided to fly back, and had traveled as far as Abilene, Texas, before crashing during a takeoff maneuver. She had been close to the crowd, and pieces of debris landed on the crowd and on their cars nearby. She was officially reprimanded, both by the press and by the Department of Commerce, which felt that she had put spectators at risk. A replacement autogiro was flown out, and she arrived back in Newark on June 22.

Amelia continued to perform stunts and demonstrations in the autogiro. In early September she was performing at an air show in Detroit when the autogiro crashed during a landing attempt. The aircraft was destroyed, but Amelia emerged unhurt from the accident.

FLYING SOLO

With the autogiro gone, Amelia began looking about for a new project. She had been working on a new book, but was tired from the strenuous lecture tours and of telling what seemed to her to be the same story over and over. She wanted a new adventure. She also had always felt as if part of her fame had been earned more from chance than from her own efforts. She had become the first woman to cross the Atlantic, but others had piloted the plane. She had only gone along for the ride.

For some time she had considered the possibility of once more crossing the Atlantic, but this time flying herself. By 1932, she was ready. She had a new plane—a red and gold Lockheed Vega—that was fully capable of making the crossing. She knew that other women were planning to attempt the trip—she wanted to be the first. She discussed the plan with Bernt Balchen, a Norwegian pilot who had accompanied Roald Amundsen on his 1926 North Pole flight in a dirigible, and had served as pilot on Richard Byrd's South Pole expedition in 1929. Balchen agreed that Amelia was ready, and offered to serve as her technical adviser.

To avoid attracting attention to the project before they were ready, Amelia officially loaned her new Vega to Balchen, allowing the rumors to spread that Balchen would be using the plane for his own flight with Lincoln Ellsworth to the South Pole. Balchen set to work, taking the plane to New Jersey's Teterboro Airport to begin preparing it for the flight. Amelia had been flying the plane for nearly three years. It needed some tuning to be in shape for the long flight. A Lockheed mechanic was hired to assist in the preparations, and for the next two months a new engine and additional fuel tanks were installed, two new compasses were added, the ailerons (the surfaces near the trailing edge of the wings that were critical for maneuvers) were replaced, and the instrument panel was supplemented by a new drift indicator and directional gyrocompass. The new fuel tanks increased the plane's fuel capacity to 420 gallons (1,590 liters), making it possible for it to travel about 3,200 miles (5,150 kilometers).

In addition to preparing her plane for the difficult flight, Amelia had to prepare herself. While continuing to work on her new book and keep up with her lecture schedule, she added training in instrument navigation and weather training, skills that would be critical to a solo flight. Amelia would be navigating a good portion of the flight "blind" through fog and darkness. Her skills using her instruments to navigate would mean the difference between life and death.

It was April when Amelia began her preparations, and by mid-May she was studying maps forecasting weather patterns over the Atlantic. She enlisted the assistance of Dr. James H. Kimball at the U.S. Weather Bureau in New York, who had

Lockheed Vega

When Amelia Earhart decided to become the first woman to fly solo across the Atlantic Ocean, the plane she chose for the flight was a Lockheed Vega 5B. The Lockheed Vega was a popular choice for pilots interested in breaking records—or setting new ones. It was a monoplane, with a streamlined design (Amelia's was bright red). Its wingspan was 41 feet (12.5 meters), and it was 8 feet, 2 inches (2.5 meters) high and 27 feet, 6 inches (8.4 meters) long. It weighed 1,650 pounds (748 kilograms).

The Vega in which Amelia would fly had been built in 1928 at the Burbank, California plant of Lockheed. Amelia purchased it on March 17, 1930, after it had been used for flying demonstrations. In September 1930, while Amelia was testing it in Virginia, her backrest collapsed. She fell backward into the plane's cabin, and the Vega's fuselage was damaged during the sudden landing. Repairs took more than a year.

To prepare the plane for the transatlantic flight, Amelia's technical adviser, Bernt Balchen, overhauled the Vega, strengthening its fuselage to accommodate additional fuel tanks and installing additional instruments to aid in navigation. The preparations were carried out in secret; most people believed that Balchen was tuning up the Vega for his own expedition.

On May 20, 1932, Amelia set off, alone in the Lockheed Vega, from Newfoundland. She flew for 14 hours and 54 minutes before finally reaching Northern Ireland after a 2,026-mile (3,260-kilometer) flight, becoming the first woman—and the second person—to fly solo across the Atlantic.

In June 1933, Amelia Earhart sold the Lockheed Vega to the Franklin Institute in Philadelphia. It was on display there until 1966, when it was moved to the Smithsonian Institution in Washington, D.C.

provided valuable advice on the timing of her first transatlantic flight. She had planned her departure for May 20, but the weather for that period made the trip look doubtful.

On the morning of May 20, Amelia went out to Teterboro Airport to discuss the plans with Balchen and practice a bit of flying. Just before noon, her husband phoned. He was in Kimball's office, and they were studying the weather maps. There was now clear weather over the Atlantic, with good visibility all the way to Harbor Grace in Newfoundland. Amelia conferred with Balchen, and they agreed that she should take advantage of the good weather.

She drove quickly to her home in Rye, New York, and changed into her "flying uniform"—riding jodhpurs, a windbreaker, and a silk shirt. She packed her leather flying suit, as well as maps, a comb, a toothbrush, and a thermos with tomato juice. She was back at the airport before 3:00 P.M., and within 20 minutes she was in the air. Balchen was flying while her mechanic, Eddie Gorski, and Amelia rested in the cabin. When they arrived at Harbor Grace, Amelia rested a bit more while Balchen and Gorski made last-minute adjustments to the plane.

She was awakened around 6:30 P.M. and told that the plane was ready. After a few final instructions and a handshake with Balchen and Gorski, she climbed into the Vega. The sun was just setting. It was 7:12 P.M. on May 20, 1932. Five year earlier, Charles Lindbergh had become the first person to cross the Atlantic. Now Amelia Earhart was attempting to become the first woman to make that same solo journey.

ACROSS THE ATLANTIC AGAIN

The first few hours of the flight were uneventful. The moon rose over a low bank of clouds as Amelia soared along at 12,000 feet (3,658 meters). Then disaster struck. Her altimeter—the instrument that shows the pilot his or her height above the

In 1931 Amelia was a married woman, but she was no less focused on her career as a pilot. The publisher George Putnam was both her husband and her most enthusiastic supporter.

ground—failed. The dials on the altimeter simply swung back and forth, uselessly.

It was a frightening moment, but George Putnam later wrote that Amelia felt at that moment not fear, but rather awe. She would need to make the rest of the flight without any sense of how high she was traveling.

The moon disappeared behind some clouds, and a lightning storm shook the plane. Amelia struggled to maintain control in the darkness as lightning flashed around her. Finally, she saw a break in the clouds and flew through that gap and up toward where she hoped the moon would give more light, above the clouds.

For 30 minutes the plane climbed—she was able to record the climb using the barograph, which measures the plane's climb and descent. The Lockheed's wings grew heavy. Amelia could see ice on the wings, and then slush on the window. Just as Amelia was processing the information that she had picked up ice, the plane went into a sudden spin. The barometers showed that the plane at one point was dropping vertically 3,000 feet (914 meters). Amelia wrestled with the controls as the plane plummeted. The plane continued to spin, rushing downward, until the lower temperatures below the clouds melted the ice. She finally was able to regain control of the plane. As she righted the aircraft, she looked below and could see the whitecaps of the ocean. She had regained control just in time.

Another frightening moment in the flight came when the plane's exhaust manifold seam parted, the result of a bad weld. Feeling the vibration, Amelia looked over the instrument panel and could see the glow of flames trailing out. The flames themselves did not frighten her—they were to be expected as the fuel and air burned under pressure—but they looked much worse at night and the damage from them might cause serious problems. Throughout the night, the manifold continued to vibrate, increasingly louder and the shaking more noticeable.

The sun eventually rose, and Amelia was soon flying just inside of the top of the clouds to help protect her tired eyes from the brilliant reflection of the sun. She had seen only one ship below, going out of Harbor Grace. She blinked the plane's navigation lights, but was not certain whether any ships below could see her.

Two hours from her planned destination—Valencia Island in the southwestern part of Ireland—she turned on her reserve fuel tank. At this moment, she discovered yet another unwelcome piece of news: her fuel gauge was leaking. Fuel was steadily dripping into the cockpit, much of it onto her left shoulder. The exhaust manifold was still burning, the vibration was increasing, and now fumes from the leaking fuel could at any moment explode from the flames of the exhaust system. Amelia decided at that point that she would land as soon as she could, wherever she could. She was concerned about missing Ireland altogether, so she swung the plane slightly northeast.

Finally, she saw below her a small fishing vessel. She circled above, in part so that it would be clear that she had made it at least that far, should something happen to the plane before she reached land. The ship below set off some kind of smoke signal to indicate that she had been spotted, and she flew on another 100 miles (161 kilometers) before reaching the coast.

When Amelia finally spotted land, she had no idea where she was, what the weather would be like, or whether there was any danger from mountains or other obstacles ahead. She saw a railroad below and followed it, thinking that it might lead to a town with an airfield. She found none and so ultimately decided to put down in a large pasture. A single farmer was the only witness to the end of Amelia's historic flight. He walked over as Amelia wearily climbed out of the plane. "I've come from America!" she told him. "Have you now?" he responded mildly.

In fact, Amelia was in Teelin Head, in County Donegal, the northwest corner of Ireland. She was some 200 miles (322 kilometers) north of where she had planned to land. As a small crowd of curious people began to gather around the plane, Amelia hitched a ride to the nearest house with a telephone, about six miles away. She called Putnam and shared the happy news that she had arrived safely on the other side of the Atlantic.

It was Saturday, May 21, 1932. Amelia Earhart had flown

A crowd gathered in Londonderry, Northern Ireland, on May 22, 1932, as Amelia took off for London. She was now officially the first woman to fly solo across the Atlantic Ocean.

2,026 miles (3,260 kilometers) in 14 hours and 54 minutes. She had been the first woman to cross the Atlantic. Now she was the first woman to cross the Atlantic solo, and the only person to fly across the Atlantic twice.

ON TO LONDON

Amelia spent the night at the home of the farmer who owned the pasture where she had landed. She was exhausted from her long flight. But the next day she traveled on to the Associated Press office in Londonderry, where messages of congratulations awaited her. There were telegrams from her sister and mother, from the American president Herbert Hoover, a message from King George and Queen Mary of England, and even a cable from her dry cleaner.

She continued on to London, where the American ambassador invited her to stay at the embassy. She needed to borrow some clothes from the ambassador's wife before she was able to make a quick shopping trip. She had arrived only with the clothes she was wearing to fly, and the many luncheons and dinners to which she was invited in London required a more extensive wardrobe than jodhpurs and a leather flying jacket. She was presented with an honorary membership in the British Guild of Airpilots and Navigators, becoming only the second non-British citizen to be given that certificate.

George Putnam sailed across the Atlantic and Amelia went with him to Paris, where she attended air races, laid a wreath at the Tomb of the Unknown Soldier, and was presented with the French Cross of the Legion of Honor. The couple was next invited to Rome, where they met with both the pope and Mussolini. In Brussels, they met the king and queen of Belgium. At each stop, Amelia was presented with awards and honors; in every city crowds surrounded her wherever she went. She had become an international celebrity.

Finally, on June 15, after one final reception in France's port city of Le Havre, George and Amelia set sail on the *Ile de France*, headed for New York. Crowds lined the quays to see her off, and three airplanes flew above the ship, escorting it out to the ocean and dropping flowers on board in her honor.

Back in New York, Amelia embarked on yet another whirlwind follow-up to her flight. There was a ticker-tape parade in her honor in New York City, complete with a speech by the mayor and complimentary speeches by other famous aviators. Then it was on to Washington, D.C., where the National Geographic Society honored Amelia with its special gold medal—she was the first woman to be given that honor. The

Thousands of people lined the parade route in New York City to welcome Amelia home after her solo transatlantic flight. Mayor James Walker greeted her in a ceremony at the city hall plaza.

awards ceremony was broadcast by NBC to its radio affiliates across the country. The U.S. Senate awarded Amelia the Distinguished Flying Cross, and she was hosted at a formal dinner at the White House with President Hoover and his wife.

There were many other cities, and many other awards

ceremonies, including the prestigious presentation of an honorary membership in the National Aeronautic Association, an honor given to only 14 men before. Amelia's new book, *The Fun of It*, with its final chapter detailing her experiences flying across the Atlantic, was published and became an instant best-seller.

In July, Amelia flew to California to attend the 1932 Summer Olympic Games. She was planning to then fly back east and decided to attempt to become the first woman to fly non-stop coast to coast. But she was forced to make a landing in Columbus, Ohio. When she finally reached her destination—Newark, New Jersey—she had managed to break one record: Her flying time was better than that of any other female pilot flying coast to coast. The previous best time had been set by Ruth Nichols—a coast-to-coast crossing of 29 hours, 1 minute, and 49 seconds. Amelia reached the coast (although not non-stop) in 19 hours, 14 minutes, and 40 seconds, nearly 10 hours faster than Nichols's time. She returned to California for a few more days at the Olympic Games, before once more deciding to try to make the nonstop flight. On August 25 she succeeded, becoming the first woman to fly nonstop coast to coast and breaking her own record time by making the trip in 19 hours and 5 minutes.

AT THE WHITE HOUSE

Amelia had visited the White House as a guest of President Hoover following her return from her solo trip across the Atlantic. George Putnam had found the Hoovers gracious but their home a bit "gloomy." The Putnams had quite a different impression of the next inhabitants of the White House—Franklin and Eleanor Roosevelt. They were frequent guests of the Roosevelts.

In April 1933 Amelia was a guest at the White House when Eleanor Roosevelt mentioned that she had never flown at night.

Amelia loved night flying—the magic of viewing the lights of stars above and the lights of the city below—and wanted the first lady to share that experience. She quickly telephoned a contact at Eastern Airlines and arranged to borrow a plane. Still dressed in their long satin evening gowns, Amelia and Eleanor climbed into the borrowed plane and flew up over Washington.

A more serious moment came the next day, when Amelia was invited to speak before 3,000 members of the Daughters of the American Revolution. The group had been demonstrating in favor of building up America's weapons arsenal in light of the unsettling developments in Europe (in the years just before World War II). Amelia had experienced the effects of war as a nurse dealing with battle-scarred soldiers in Canada, and what she had seen had transformed her into a committed pacifist. She bravely addressed that large crowd, criticizing them for speaking out in favor of rearming America without taking any steps to ensure an equal role for women in the military. Amelia pointed out the hypocrisy in their position to the startled audience: unless they planned to make use of the weapons themselves, by fighting for their country, they had no business in taking a position so strongly in favor of rearmament.

Amelia was gradually becoming a spokesperson for political causes, as well as for aviation. But as she traveled around the country, making speeches and writing articles, she was contemplating what next challenge might await her.

The Pacific Challenge

On July 1, 1933, Amelia participated in the Bendix Transcontinental Air Derby. There were only two female contestants in the race—Amelia and Ruth Nichols. The two had enjoyed a rivalry dating back to Amelia's earliest flying days in 1922. Ruth had broken the first record set by Amelia in 1922 and had been one of the candidates to serve on the Guest expedition across the Atlantic that made Amelia famous. She had continued to quietly advance the cause of women aviators, though she lacked the drive for headlines that helped make Amelia the most famous female pilot of that time. They also happened to be neighbors, both living in the town of Rye, New York.

Both were also highly skilled and highly competitive. In the Bendix race, the two women were competing for a prize of $2,500. The race also had four male pilots, who would share a prize of $9,000, with the winner receiving a $1,000 bonus if he broke the record of 12 hours and 39 minutes for flying west.

Amelia flew her red Lockheed Vega, taking off from Newark on July 1, stopping overnight in Kansas before arriving in third place at the final destination of Los Angeles. She arrived nearly a full day before Nichols, returning to Newark and breaking yet

Beneath her casual style and easygoing smile, Amelia was a competitive and proficient pilot who continually sought new challenges.

another record, this time her own, by making the return trip in 17 hours, 7 minutes, and 30 seconds.

At the age of 37, Amelia was perhaps the world's most famous female pilot. She had set records and then broken them again and again. She had flown across the country and across the Atlantic Ocean. She was in demand as an author and speaker. But the quiet life, enjoying the fame of earlier successes, was not one that suited her. She was constantly looking for new challenges, new ways to test herself, and in 1934 she found the next adventure.

ACROSS THE PACIFIC

On January 11, 1934, a group of six U.S. Navy planes set a new record, becoming the first team to travel from California to Hawaii, flying for a total of 24 hours and 45 minutes. It was an impressive accomplishment, adding to the list of those who had crossed portions of the Pacific in previous years. In 1928 a team led by Sir Charles Kingsford-Smith had flown from Oakland, California, to Brisbane, Australia. In 1931 a two-man crew—Hugh Herndon Jr. and Clyde Pangborn— successfully crossed the Pacific nonstop from Tokyo to Wenatchee, Washington.

Several teams had crossed the Pacific, but no one had managed to fly solo between Hawaii and the West Coast. Amelia wanted to be the first to make that 2,400-mile (3,862-kilometer) trip. Amelia spent several months completing her scheduled lectures and appearances, then in August spent one month with Putnam on vacation in Wyoming. By the fall, the couple had moved to Los Angeles. Putnam was now working for Paramount Pictures, and Amelia felt that basing herself on the West Coast would make preparations for the Pacific flight easier. The Lockheed factory was in nearby Burbank, and Amelia wanted to overhaul her plane and make sure that it was operating in optimal condition.

In California, Amelia began to work with Paul Mantz, a 31-year-old former army pilot. Mantz had met George Putnam first, working with him on a movie Paramount made called *Wings*, which won an Academy Award for Best Picture in 1927 for its exciting depiction of aviation. Mantz was a skilled stunt flyer—he had performed some of the dogfights in *Wings* himself—but he was also an expert technician who quickly became a helpful adviser to Amelia as she made her preparations for the flight from Hawaii to California.

On December 22, the Putnams and Paul Mantz and his wife set sail for Hawaii. Rumors were beginning to circulate that Amelia was going to attempt the transpacific flight, but Amelia tried to squash them by stating that the trip was to give a series of lectures and to make some flights around the islands.

Few people were fooled, and criticism began to mount that Amelia's plan was too dangerous for any man or woman to attempt solo. The newspapers published reports that her plane was too small to safely make the flight. In November, a three-man crew led by Captain Charles Ulm had attempted to make the flight from Oakland to Honolulu but had disappeared somewhere off the coast of Oahu. For a month, U.S. Army, U.S. Navy, and U.S. Coast Guard vessels, as well as numerous fishing boats, had combed the seas near where the last contact—an SOS—was given, but they turned up nothing. Many critics pointed out that Amelia was risking her life at public expense—should she fail, another expensive search would need to be undertaken, and the image of aviation safety would be seriously damaged by the loss of a prominent aviator.

The navy, responding to the criticism, refused to clear Amelia's plane for departure, stating that her plane's radio did not have the necessary range for safety—the ability to transmit 2,500 miles (4,023 kilometers) to Los Angeles. Amelia protested, replying that she had spoken with a radio operator as far away as Kingman, Arizona. When the navy expressed disbelief, Mantz took matters into his own hands. He took the plane up to 12,000 feet (3,658 meters) and contacted Kingman, Arizona, himself. The navy ultimately agreed to clear the flight.

The next obstacle came from the organization that had agreed to sponsor Amelia's flight—a group of sugarcane and pineapple growers, as well as other businessmen, had offered a $10,000 prize for the first solo flight. The businessmen had launched a campaign in the U.S. Congress to reduce the tax on sugar, but the criticism of Amelia's plans had prompted them to consider backing out of the competition, fearing the bad publicity should her plane be lost. Amelia faced them down, telling members of the association's committee that she could smell the "aroma of cowardice" in the room. Then she made it clear that she would make the flight—with or without the prize money. The prize offer was quickly reinstated.

It was then merely a matter of waiting for the right kind of weather. For several days dim forecasts and torrential downpours kept Amelia grounded in Hawaii. Finally, on the afternoon of January 11, 1935, the conditions were right.

ALONE OVER THE PACIFIC

The rain had been heavy that morning, but by 4:00 P.M. it had stopped. In less than half an hour, Amelia and George were at the hangar at the U.S. Army's Wheeler Field. The "official" story was that Amelia would be attempting only a small test flight, so few people had gathered to watch Amelia take off.

The plane had been loaded with 500 gallons (1,893 liters) of fuel, enough to successfully make the crossing. The Vega had also been equipped with additional radio and navigational aids, an inflatable raft, and a bright red inflatable life vest for Amelia. With the fuel and extra equipment, the plane weighed more than 6,000 pounds (2,296 kilograms), but

Amelia was draped with traditional leis when she arrived by boat in Hawaii. She was scheduled to fly her Lockheed Vega from Honolulu across the Pacific Ocean to Oakland, California.

Mantz and Amelia felt that it would be able to take off in approximately 3,000 feet (914 meters). Wheeler Field's grass takeoff strip was twice that length, and the Army had planted small flags labeled with the distance along the runway to help Amelia gauge her liftoff.

Amelia climbed on board, wearing a lined flying suit for warmth. She gunned the engine, then signaled to the ground crew below to remove the giant blocks restraining the wheels. The Vega began to roll down the runway, gradually picking up speed until taking off at precisely 3,000 feet (914 meters). Amelia could see the anxious faces below as she headed up into the sky. At 4:44 P.M. she was on her way—attempting to become the first person ever to fly solo across the Pacific Ocean.

While Amelia had a matter-of-fact approach to her flight, it was clear that she had some unspoken fears. In the letter she left behind for George, she was no doubt conscious of her legacy: "If I do not do a good job, it will not be because the plane and motor are not excellent nor because women cannot fly."

The new radio made a tremendous difference to Amelia throughout the course of this flight—and to the fans who learned of her departure later that night and then anxiously awaited word of her safe arrival. At approximately quarter-to and quarter-after each hour, Amelia made regular radio contact. She did not give out her position, but reassured the listeners with the constant message that everything was fine. She did report her altitude and the speed at which she was flying, as well as the two ships she saw below. To maintain radio contact, she needed to reel a long antenna in and out of the cabin floor, but it was a help to her to maintain the contact—and she could listen to radio broadcasts from various stations on the mainland as she traveled.

Eighteen hours after leaving Honolulu, Amelia spotted the California coast. She could see the San Francisco Bay below, and so turned north toward her targeted destination: Oakland. There had been some uncertainty about whether she would land at Los Angeles or San Francisco, but at approximately 7:55 A.M. on January 12, she announced that she was on course and would be heading for Oakland. At the news, a crowd of nearly 10,000 began to gather at the Oakland Airport.

Her red plane came in low and fast, landing so far down the runway that at first the crowd did not even notice her. Then a siren was sounded on the airfield, Amelia revved the engines and turned the plane toward the hangar. The crowd immediately rushed toward her. The cockpit door opened and a tired but smiling Amelia appeared. She was showered with roses before she was finally rescued by a group of mechanics, who literally pulled her plane into the hangar by its wings and then locked the doors behind them. Amelia was taken to an Oakland hotel for some much-needed rest.

With that flight she achieved two new "firsts." She became the first person to fly solo across the Pacific, and she was the first person to fly solo across both the Atlantic and Pacific.

SOUTH OF THE BORDER

An important change had taken place in Amelia's career with her arrival in Oakland. She had been a skilled pilot in her earlier years of flying, but much of her success had been as much due to Putnam's efforts to publicize her flights as to the flights themselves. The Pacific flight marked a critical turning point for Amelia. The flight had marked a first—for any pilot, male or female. She had done it not because of luck or good timing—although these had been important—but thanks to careful planning, skilled assistance, and her own piloting.

Shortly after her arrival, Amelia was invited to come to Mexico by the Mexican president Lázaro Cárdenas. She would not be the first pilot to fly from the United States to Mexico City—Charles Lindbergh had made the flight from Washington, D.C., to Mexico City in 1927—but the flight would offer an opportunity to set other records. Amelia hoped to become the first pilot to travel from Los Angeles to Mexico City, and then the first to fly from Mexico City to Newark, New Jersey.

Little more than three months after her historic Pacific flight, Amelia was once more in the air. Just before midnight on April 19, Amelia took off from the Burbank airfield. About 50 miles (80 kilometers) outside Mexico City she was forced to land. She had lost her way, and finally found some people near the village of Nopala who directed her by pointing. She took off again and arrived in the Mexican capital. The flight from California to Mexico took a little more than 13 and a half hours.

She was treated like a honored guest, and a round of fiestas

Mexico City was the destination for Amelia in April 1935. After landing first in a Mexican village, she eventually arrived in the Mexican capital, where she was the focus of fiestas and celebrations.

and celebrations marked her time in Mexico. Amelia had hoped to use her visit as an opportunity to meet with Mexican working women, to learn about their working conditions and share her own views on the importance of independence and greater self-sufficiency. But for the most part she was rushed from one gala to the next, hosted by both Mexicans and the American expatriates living south of the border.

Amelia had hoped to make a fairly rapid return trip, but weather conditions kept her in Mexico until May 8. Early that morning, her weather adviser, Doc Kimball, had informed her that the weather looked promising, with decent visibility although the winds were not very favorable. Just after 6 A.M. Mexican time, the Vega rolled down the runway. Takeoff was more difficult because of the location—8,000 feet (2,438 meters) above sea level—but finally the heavy plane lifted off. The 2,125-mile (3,420-kilometer) flight was uneventful, and Amelia reached Newark Airport after a nonstop flight of 14 hours and 18 minutes. A huge crowd was waiting to greet her. Yet another record had been broken, and Amelia held another first.

ACADEMICS AND AVIATION

In the fall of 1935, Amelia also began serving as a lecturer at Purdue University in Indiana. She served as a visiting faculty member and as a consultant to the university's career services for women program. The position required her to be on campus only a few weeks each year, but gave her an opportunity to further promote careers in aviation to women.

Purdue had its own small airfield, as well as an aeronautics department. As Amelia discussed with the university's president, Dr. Edward Elliott, the scope of her role on campus, it became clear that the collaboration might provide both Amelia and Purdue with an opportunity to focus on the potential for aviation research. Elliott began to approach friends of the university to seek donations for what would become the "Amelia Earhart Fund for Aeronautical Research." Ultimately, more than $50,000 was raised.

The sum was to be used to purchase a kind of "flying laboratory," a bigger plane than Amelia had previously flown. On March 20, 1936, an order was placed at the Lockheed factory for the aircraft that would become Amelia's laboratory. It was an Electra, a two-motored, dual-control monoplane. The Electra could reach an altitude of 27,000 feet (8,229 meters)

Milestones in Aviation

1903	Wilbur and Orville Wright build the first successful airplane
1927	Charles Lindbergh makes the first solo transatlantic flight
1928	**Amelia Earhart becomes the first woman to fly across the Atlantic Ocean**
1932	**Amelia Earhart becomes the first woman to make a solo transatlantic flight**
1935	**Amelia Earhart makes the first solo flight across the Pacific Ocean**
1947	Chuck Yeager pilots the first aircraft to travel at the speed of sound
1957	*Sputnik 1* is the first artificial satellite
1962	*Apollo 11* makes the first manned lunar landing
1976	*Viking Lander* is the first spacecraft to operate on the surface of Mars
1983	*Pioneer 10* is the first spacecraft to leave the earth's solar system
1999	*Breitling Orbiter 3 Gondola* makes the first nonstop balloon flight around the world

and was capable of traveling up to 210 miles (338 kilometers) per hour. It could seat up to 10 passengers.

But there would be no additional passengers traveling on this plane. Amelia, with the help of her adviser Paul Mantz, had other plans for the "flying laboratory." The seats would be removed and their space occupied by auxiliary fuel tanks as well as additional technical equipment.

The plane would be outfitted to travel nearly 4,500 miles (7,242 kilometers) nonstop. Amelia was planning a new trip—this time around the world.

Around the World

A melia had been dreaming of a flight around the world for several years before she actually began serious preparations. It would not be the first such flight—a U.S. Army Air Service team had traveled around the world in 1924, and aviator Wiley Post had made the trip twice—once in 1931 and again 1933.

But Amelia wanted to be the first woman to travel around the world. In addition, she wanted to make the trip using a different route from those traveled by previous aviators. In the past, the goal of those flying around the world had not merely been to make the trip, but to make it in the fastest time. For this reason, the shortest possible distances had been mapped out, and this had been the route the aviators had followed.

Amelia had a different idea. She decided that she would not attempt to break the existing records for the fastest trip around the globe. Instead, she would travel the world close to the equator, the midpoint of the globe, creating the longest possible distance. Her stated goal in the trip, when she finally announced that she was planning it, was both for her own personal desire and also to advance the cause of aviation by checking and reporting on how the equipment would respond to the difficult challenges such a long flight would create.

The route she would follow soon took shape, both in her thoughts and then on paper. She would travel from Oakland to Honolulu, then to Howland Island in the south-central Pacific, and then to Australia. Next she would fly over India and on to Arabia (now Saudi Arabia), then Africa, across the South Atlantic and on to Brazil. The last leg of the journey would be from Brazil to New York.

George Putnam and Amelia discussed the plans for Amelia's trip around the world in a hangar where her Lockheed Electra was being prepared for flight.

The planning was ultimately highly critical. Each destination would present its own special set of challenges and circumstances. Fuel supplies would need to be arranged ahead of time, weather conditions would have to be carefully plotted all along the route, suitable landing points would need to be located. Many of the places where she would set down lacked rudimentary materials necessary for flying, and Amelia and her consultants would have to prepare for many different eventualities well before the plane first took off.

Particular attention was given to the radio equipment Amelia would carry on board. The radio had been a critical factor in the success of her flight across the Pacific, and Amelia wanted to have the latest version available for this more difficult journey. She received from Western Electric a 50-watt radio transmitter and an adjustable, four-band receiver with remote-control operation. The radio could transmit on three frequencies: 6,210 kHz during the day and 3,105 kHz at night—the standard frequencies for all airplanes—plus offered the addition of an emergency frequency at 500 kHz. The emergency frequency required a 250-foot (76-meter) trailing aerial in order to operate effectively. The aerial was heavy—it had to be reeled in and out using a handle—but it could provide a useful lifeline in the event of an emergency.

The Lockheed Electra was equipped with a number of special features to make it suitable for the round-the-world trip. There were wing deicers, instruments to assist in minimal visibility situations, a fuel minimizer, and extra fuel tanks—three on each wing and six more in the fuselage.

On August 29, 1936, Amelia decided to take the new Lockheed Electra on a test flight. She entered the plane in the Bendix Trophy race, and flew from California to New York, where the race would begin, using the coast-to-coast trip as a trial to sort out any problems. There were several minor incidents, including trouble with the fuel lines, and Amelia's performance in the race was poor.

PREPARING FOR THE JOURNEY

The team Amelia assembled to prepare for the flight were old friends as well as experts in their respective fields. Paul Mantz would serve once more as Amelia's technical adviser, and Bo McKneely would serve as full-time mechanic. For the critical role of navigator, Amelia chose Harry Manning, a skilled mariner who Amelia had known since 1928. Manning was also a ham radio operator and a pilot.

Manning's navigational skills would be critical at certain stages of the trip. Parts of the Pacific Ocean were not well charted, and there were many small islands whose location and distance would need to be researched to plot out the plane's course.

In February 1937, Amelia officially announced that she was preparing for a round-the-world flight. Appearing at the press conference in a dark-blue wool dress with a bright scarf wrapped around her neck, she used a globe as a prop, pointing out the route she planned to fly. The trip, she announced, would be approximately 27,000 miles (43,451 kilometers).

As final preparations were made, the team—Amelia, plus Mantz, Manning, and McKneely—continued to debate several of the details. One of the greatest concerns was the choice of Howland Island as a landing spot along the way. The island had been chosen because of its convenient location—about halfway between Hawaii and New Guinea. It would give Amelia a critical resting point, as well as provide a fuel stop. The U.S. Department of Commerce had built a new emergency landing field, which would be available for Amelia to use.

But the island was small—only 2 miles (3 kilometers) long and a half-mile (.80 kilometers) wide. It was 40 miles (64 kilometers) away from any other land, and its highest point was no more than 18 feet (5 meters). It would take a highly skilled navigator to locate this pinprick in the middle of the Pacific.

While Manning was confident, his primary experience had been in naval, rather than aerial, navigation. It was decided to add one more navigator to the team—Frederick Noonan. He had served as a navigator on Pan American's routes across the Pacific. Noonan was familiar with the region and its problems, and he had extensive experience in aerial navigation.

Noonan had helped map out Pan Am's air routes to Hawaii, Guam, Hong Kong, and the Philippines. He had worked both as a navigator and navigation teacher. But he had recently stepped down from his work at Pan Am, determined to start his own navigation school. He was also rumored to have a problem with alcohol.

It was finally decided that different members of the team would fly with her at different stages, depending on the requirements of each leg of the journey. Amelia, of course, would fly the entire route. Mantz would travel with the team to Honolulu. Noonan would travel with Amelia as far as Howland Island. Manning would go on to Australia, and Amelia would make the final leg of the trip alone.

For several weeks, heavy rain battered Oakland, the point from which Amelia planned to depart. The conditions were so unfavorable—the unpaved runway at Oakland Airport had turned to mud—that Amelia hesitated to even set an official departure date. It was simply a matter of waiting, and then waiting some more.

TAKING OFF

At last, on March 17, 1937, the weather cleared. Shortly after 4:30 P.M., the Electra was brought out of its hangar. A 7,000-foot (2,134-meter) runway had been constructed specifically for the plane, and after running several engine checks, Paul Mantz brought the plane to the head of the long runway. Amelia appeared and climbed into the pilot's seat. Mantz moved to his position on her right. In the back, seated at a special navigation table, were Manning and Noonan. The table had been bolted down to the floor of the plane's cabin, and it

Paul Mantz was the technical adviser for the round-the-world flight. Mantz argued for more time to prepare for the flight and was especially concerned about the plane's radio equipment.

was equipped with all of the latest navigation tools, including chronometers in rubber mounts, altimeters, airspeed and drift indicators, and a temperature gauge.

They had attempted the takeoff for several days in a row, so there were few people on hand to witness what many believed would be yet another failed attempt to get underway. But within minutes Amelia had revved the engines, gained the clearance from the control tower, and the Electra was quickly in the air.

At 5:40 A.M. local time, the unmistakable silhouette of Diamond Head appeared below. In 15 hours and 47 minutes, Amelia and her crew landed at Wheeler Field in Honolulu. It was a record-breaking time for the east to west journey. The flight had been smooth, although Amelia was tired and anxious about the navigational difficulties the next leg of the journey—from Honolulu to Howland Island—presented. Their departure had to be delayed by one day, due to bad weather.

This next leg of the journey would be shorter than the one Amelia had just completed. Howland Island was more than 1,800 miles (2,897 kilometers) away. Amelia requested that the plane be loaded with 900 gallons (3,407 liters) of fuel, much more than was needed, but Amelia wanted to make sure that there was enough for her to return to Hawaii if the conditions became too difficult to make a landing at Howland.

The Electra was moved from Wheeler Field to Luke Field, where a 3,000-foot (914-meter) paved runway would make the takeoff easier. As dawn slowly came, lightening the sky over Pearl Harbor, the crew made their final check. Mantz was now an observer, watching the others climb into the Electra. At 7:35 A.M. Amelia signaled to the ground crew to remove the chocks—the concrete blocks that blocked the movement of the wheels.

Amelia gunned the motors and slowly the Electra moved down the runway, gathering speed. About 1,000 feet (305 meters) down the runway, disaster struck. Amelia recalled that it felt as if the plane suddenly pulled to her right. She reduced the power on the opposite engine, and was able to swing the plane from moving to the right back to the left. She thought this would help her to regain control of the plane and straighten it out. Instead, it continued to swing in a giant arc to the left, its heavy weight propelling it on in a ground loop. As the plane swung, the right wheel and undercarriage were torn off, and it raced down the runway on its bottom. Gasoline began to pour out, and a shower of sparks rained down.

Amelia quickly cut the engine, undoubtedly preventing a fire or explosion. Ambulances and fire trucks went racing down the runway as a shaken Manning, Noonan, and Amelia climbed out of the plane.

The damaged Electra would require extensive repairs before it could fly again. Amelia made the necessary arrangements for the plane to be returned to the Lockheed factory in Burbank. She reassured the gathering of reporters that the flight would continue. This was merely a temporary setback.

NEW PARTS AND NEW PLANS

When the Electra was once more at the Lockheed factory, Amelia learned that repairs would take at least five weeks. The damaged parts would need to be replaced, and some parts would need to be redesigned to accommodate the extra equipment and fuel—and the weight they would add. The cost would be $25,000.

The March flight had been planned to take advantage of weather conditions along the route. With the flight now postponed until May, a new route had to be devised and new arrangements made to position fuel and supplies along the way. All of this would cost money, and Amelia and George had tapped extensively into their own personal funds. The successful completion of the trip would provide them with income from Amelia's prearranged published accounts of the trip, plus speaking engagements and other projects. But the money was needed now to cover the cost of supplies and repairs. George set to work raising the additional sums, while Amelia and her crew mapped out their new route. Amelia also prepared the beginning chapters of the book that would relay the details of her journey, to be called *World Flight*. She planned to make notes as she traveled and then mail them to her husband, who would have them typed and waiting for her. In that way, her notes would be ready and waiting for the final draft, so that the book could be quickly published after the trip was over.

Changing weather conditions along the route now presented new problems. To solve these, the round-the-world trip was reversed for its planned takeoff in late May. This time Amelia would fly east, from Oakland to Miami and then on to South America. She would cross Africa and then fly to Australia. From Australia she would travel on to New Guinea and then, at the end of the trip, she would make the crossing over the south-central Pacific and, the most technically difficult point, the stop at Howland Island. Finally she would go on to Honolulu and then return to Oakland.

Harry Manning had taken only a three-month leave from his job, and so as the repairs to the Electra were completed, it became clear that he would have to return to work. It was decided that Noonan would take his place as navigator for the entire trip. There were also problems with the radio equipment—problems that had concerned Paul Mantz. He felt that the equipment needed much more extensive testing, and he was worried at the pace at which the trip was being hastily put together. He was even more concerned when he learned that the 250-foot (76-meter) radio antenna—the one to be used in the event of an emergency—had been removed on Amelia's directions. She felt that the antenna would be too difficult to reel in and out, but it would leave a dangerous gap in communications during the long period of travel across the south-central Pacific.

On May 18 the newly repaired and rebuilt Electra was delivered to Amelia. Mantz and Amelia made some small test flights, checking out the plane's capacity. But the two had several disagreements over minor points in the plane's preparations, and when Mantz left for a two-day trip to St. Louis he believed that Amelia would continue in preflight preparations for another week. He was shocked to learn that she had made her own plans, without him.

Technical adviser Paul Mantz (left) poses with Earhart and navigators Harry Manning and Fred Noonan in Honolulu in 1937. Noonan would navigate, and Amelia would pilot the ill-fated flight.

On May 21, Amelia took off on the first phase of the trip. On board with her were George Putnam, Fred Noonan, and mechanic Bo McKneely. She had made the plans with no official announcement that her journey was much more underway. The idea was that, should the Electra develop problems, she could simply return to California. Without an official announcement, there would be no problematic publicity should the plane have to go back to the Lockheed factory for additional repairs. If the flight went well, she could simply continue on her way.

But Mantz was not fooled. When he heard that Amelia's plane had taken off from Oakland, he knew that she was starting out on the flight, and this time she would do so without his advice. The reasons for this have never been made clear, but it is certain that Amelia wanted to ensure that the flight got underway as quickly as possible, while Mantz had argued for additional preparations. Amelia was concerned about the financial costs of the trip—costs that were added to with each day of delay. And so, on May 21, she set out for another attempt at the around-the-world trip.

The Electra flew from California to Tucson, Arizona, where it stopped for refueling. A small engine fire happened when Amelia tried to start the engine, but it was quickly put under control. McKneely handled the necessary repairs, and the next day they flew on to New Orleans. After an overnight stay in Louisiana, the Electra soared up over the northeast corner of the Gulf of Mexico, traveling on to Miami.

They spent a week in Miami. Amelia and McKneely worked with a team of Pan Am mechanics, testing and retesting the Electra to make it ready. There were still some problems with the radio transmissions. The issue of the 250-foot (76-meter) aerial antenna was addressed once more, and ultimately it was decided to use a shorter, more portable antenna.

Early on the morning of June 1, the Electra began its warm-up. A small crowd had gathered. Amelia sat on the wing of the plane and held her husband's hand for a few moments as the cameras clicked, recording their final goodbye. Then they moved into a nearby hangar for a more private farewell. George Putnam would later recall those last moments, as they sat on cold concrete steps holding hands: "Her eyes were clear with the light of the adventure that lay ahead. As she walked out to the great ship she seemed very small and slim and feminine, much as that littler girl must have looked years before in Kansas when she stepped forth for her first ride on the 'rolly coaster.'"

At 6:04 A.M., Amelia closed and fastened the Electra's hatch. The engine revved, the chocks were removed, and the plane began to move down the runway. Putnam stood on the roof of the airfield's administration building, watching the silver plane climb into the sky and head to the southeast, disappearing into the morning sky. It was the last time he would ever see his wife.

AROUND THE WORLD

It was now official—Amelia was once more attempting to travel around the world. Their journey would be front-page news for the next 32 days, as readers and radio listeners followed the regular updates of arrivals and departures.

For the first "official" leg of her flight, Amelia and Fred Noonan traveled to San Juan, Puerto Rico. It was a trip of 1,000 miles (1,609 kilometers), over territory familiar to Noonan, and the trip went smoothly. They traveled next to Carippito, and then on to Paramiribo, before stopping for a rest at Fortaleza. Then it was on to Natal, where they would begin their flight across the South Atlantic to Dakar, in Africa's Senegal, a distance of some 1,900 miles (3,058 kilometers).

The flight across the Atlantic took 13 hours and 12 minutes and presented few problems. The Electra was equipped with a Sperry autopilot, and at regular intervals Amelia would take a break to write down some notes in her journal while the autopilot flew. As they neared the coast of Senegal, Amelia and Noonan had a disagreement over the final navigation needed. Amelia chose to ignore Noonan's recommended adjustment to their course, and they arrived at Saint-Louis rather than Dakar, some 160 miles (257 kilometers) off course. They flew on to

Dakar the next day, where the Electra was checked and a minor repair made to the fuel meter.

The next leg of the journey took them across Africa, with stops in Gao, Fort-Lamy, El Fasher, Khartoum, and Massawa. It was a hot and long journey, and the navigation was not easy for Noonan. There were few maps available, and these generally proved to be inaccurate. Adding to the difficulty was the absence of any noticeable landmarks. But with each flight they reached their next stop with a minimum of difficulty.

Next, Amelia and Noonan set off from Africa across the Red Sea to Eritrea. They then flew down the Arabian coast to India. It was the first nonstop flight made from the Red Sea to India—another record for Amelia. In India, the Electra's fuel analyzer was replaced. It had not been operating properly and was causing Amelia some concern. After the repairs, Amelia and Noonan set off for Calcutta. The airfield had been drenched by a recent rainfall, and more rain was forecast. Amelia decided to quickly take off again, heading for Burma (now known as Myanmar). It was a difficult takeoff, the wheels sticking in the damp earth before finally the Electra was able to lift up, barely skimming over the edge of the trees lining the end of the runway.

A monsoon held the team back in Burma after their takeoff was aborted due to a heavy storm. Since leaving Miami, they had been traveling for 18 days. When the weather finally cleared, they traveled on, first to Rangoon (now known as Yangon), and then to Bangkok, Singapore, and on to Bandoeng. By now, Amelia was feeling confident in the Electra's operation and in her own abilities. She spoke with her husband and told him that she thought they would be back in California by July 4th. Putnam set to work arranging a gala welcome-home celebration for the 4th of July.

Again, weather delays prevented them from leaving Bandoeng as quickly as they had planned. Finally, on June 24, they took off for Java. But certain instruments on the Electra—

instruments critical to the conserving and monitoring of fuel—were not responding properly, and Amelia was concerned. The generator meter, the flow meter, and the fuel analyzer were all giving her problems, and she knew that these meters would be critical when she attempted the flight over the Pacific.

Amelia returned to Bandoeng for repairs to the instruments. While the Electra was being repaired, Amelia spent a few days sightseeing in nearby Jakarta. She sampled some of the local cuisine and promptly became sick with dysentery. Her poor health and equally poor weather kept the team grounded until June 27, when they finally took off for Port Darwin in Australia. Yet another repair was made at Port Darwin, this time to a blown fuse in the direction finder.

Next came a 1,200-mile (1,931-kilometer) flight to Lae in Papua New Guinea. Amelia and Noonan arrived on June 29 after a 7-hour-and-43-minute flight.

OVER THE PACIFIC

Amelia was still focused on arriving as scheduled in California on July 4th. By now, she and Noonan had traveled 22,000 miles (35,405 kilometers). Only 7,000 miles (11,265 kilometers) were left in their round-the-world journey, but these would be among the most challenging of their flight, taking them over the Pacific.

Amelia focused on removing all excess weight from the plane. Parachutes had been removed at their previous stop, in Australia, as Amelia felt that they would be of little use should the plane encounter trouble over the Pacific. The plane was packed and unpacked several times, removing every spare ounce of weight. In addition, the fuel pump and autopilot, which had been acting up, were repaired again. The oil and oil filters were changed. The engines were checked. The spark plugs were cleaned.

Amelia and Fred Noonan took a moment to pose with a local man in Lae, New Guinea, before continuing their flight. The exhausted fliers now had to concentrate on the most difficult part of the journey—from New Guinea to Howland Island.

Amelia and Noonan had been flying for a month, and by now they were both tired. In addition to handling the flying, they also had to oversee any needed repairs and refueling, plan for the next stage of the flight, and meet with reporters and local dignitaries at each of their stops. It was a grueling schedule, and photographs of the two at this point in their journey show them exhausted, with Amelia looking more tired than her navigator.

As the Electra was tuned up for this most difficult portion of the trip, Amelia and Noonan reconsidered their flight plan. Amelia had learned that the island of Narau (whose spelling has since changed to Nauru) would offer a point of bright visibility. Phosphate mines on the island ensured continued brightness even at night. The island would serve as a useful midpoint, appearing 1,400 miles (2,253 kilometers) into their 2,556-mile (4,113-kilometer) flight. They agreed to make a slight detour in their planned trip to travel over Narau, where the bright lights would give them an opportunity to check their position before continuing on to Howland Island.

Amelia estimated that the planned flight would take 18 hours. She and Noonan wanted to guarantee that they would approach Howland in the daylight, to make it easier to locate, so they needed to arrange a departure time from Lae that would ensure a daytime arrival. Amelia was also concerned about weather conditions and was focused on arriving as planned for the Independence Day celebrations.

On July 2, 1937, the weather forecast promised good visibility, although some rain squalls were predicted. Amelia felt that they were ready. At 10 A.M. local time on that Friday morning, Amelia started the Electra on its takeoff run down the 1,000-yard (914-meter) runway at Lae. It was a hot and clear day, and the plane kicked up a cloud of dust that remained long after the Electra lifted up into the sky. It was the last time Amelia Earhart would be seen.

Into
the Stars

For seven hours into her flight, Amelia maintained contact with Harry Balfour, a New Guinea Airways radio operator at Lae. Her progress and altitude were all as expected. Extensive operations had been arranged with the U.S. Coast Guard to maintain a radio network and be on alert, should the Electra encounter any unexpected trouble. Aboard the Coast Guard cutter *Ontario*, stationed along Amelia's projected route, a radio operator was standing by awaiting transmissions, while three men maintained a visual watch for her plane. They saw and heard nothing.

The Coast Guard ship *Itasca* was also attempting to track Amelia's progress. At 2:45 A.M. the radio operator on board, along with two other men, did receive a communication from the Electra, but static made it difficult to make out what was being said. The *Itasca* responded as had been arranged by broadcasting weather forecasts on the agreed-upon frequency every half-hour. There was no response, but Amelia was still thought to be a long way from the ship.

At 3:45 A.M. another message was received from Amelia,

Her Electra provides the backdrop to this pose in California, shortly before Amelia would attempt to pilot the plane around the world. George Putnam would later describe those moments as filled with anticipation of the adventure.

this one much clearer. She indicated that the weather was overcast and noted that she would listen on the hour and half-hour on a different frequency. Fifteen minutes later, the *Itasca* responded on the requested frequency, asking Amelia for her position and anticipated arrival time at Howland. There was no response.

At 4:53 A.M., the *Itasca* once more broadcast the weather when the message was interrupted by Amelia. Her message was very faint, and she was off schedule. The operator could only make out the words "partly cloudy" before the rest of her message was covered up by static.

For the next 80 minutes, the *Itasca* broadcast weather bulletins and repeatedly requested Amelia to respond with her position, but there was no response. At 6:14 A.M., 15 minutes before her scheduled arrival time at Howland, Amelia was heard again, at a louder volume, indicating that she was closer. She requested that the ship take a bearing on the Electra and indicated that she would whistle into the microphone. The whistling sound was difficult to distinguish from other radio noise, and the operators were unable to accurately pinpoint her position. Approximately 30 minutes later, which was 15 minutes past her planned arrival time at Howland, Amelia again was heard, this time at a clearer signal indicating that she was closer to the *Itasca*. Again, she requested that the ship get a bearing on the Electra; again she indicated that she would make a noise into the microphone, and this time she added that she thought she was about 100 miles out. But her whistle was too brief for operators to pinpoint her position.

At 7:42 A.M. she was heard again, and this time her signal was registered as being at the maximum reception. She is reported to have said, "We must be on you but cannot see you but gas is running low. [Some reports indicate that she said, "Only one-half hour of gas left."] Been unable to reach you by radio. We are flying at altitude one thousand feet."

The *Itasca* issued a cloud of heavy black smoke, which should have been visible for about 20 miles (32 kilometers). The sky was clear over Howland Island, but heavy clouds were visible in the northwest sky, approximately 30 miles (48 kilometers) away.

The *Itasca* decided to break with the prearranged schedule and began a constant series of transmissions on two different frequencies. One minute later Amelia was heard again, indicating for the first time that she had heard their transmission but could not locate the ship. She requested that a bearing be taken on her, but again her transmission was too brief.

For the next half-hour, the *Itasca* sent messages by voice and Morse code on all of the different frequencies that Amelia's radio was capable of receiving. There was no response. At 8:44 A.M., Amelia's voice was suddenly heard. The transmission was still at the maximum signal, but her voice sounded hurried. She attempted to give her position and indicated that she was running north and south. She noted that she would repeat the message on a different frequency. The operator on the *Itasca* immediately responded, requesting that she stay on the same frequency. But nothing further was heard.

For more than an hour, *Itasca* continued to broadcast and transmit signals, but no additional contact was made. The commander of the *Itasca* determined that Amelia probably had been forced to put down. Based on guesswork—Amelia had indicated that the sky was overcast and the only clouds nearby were to the northwest, plus had she been flying in the clearer sky over Howland she would have seen the black smoke from the ship—he ordered the vessel to proceed at full steam ahead to the north. But the extensive search that would follow would reveal nothing. Less than a month before her 40th birthday, Amelia Earhart was gone.

Amelia communicated with the U.S. Coast Guard ship *Itasca* from the cockpit of her Electra, shown here. Her last transmission was at 8:44 A.M. on July 3, 1937, after which repeated attempts to contact her went unanswered.

LOST AT SEA

For the next 16 days, Amelia would become the focus of the largest rescue attempt ever made for one lost aircraft. Some 250,000 square miles (647,500 square kilometers)—an area as large as Texas—were targeted for searching. The search party involved 65 airplanes, 10 ships, and 4,000 men. Aircraft carriers, battleships, even a British freighter and two Japanese naval vessels all helped with the search effort. But their efforts would prove fruitless. No trace of Amelia or her plane was ever found. Her disappearance would only enhance her fame. Her achievements had brought her acclaim, but the mystery of her disappearance would make her a legend.

Many theories have been discussed over the years about exactly what happened to the Electra. Conspiracy theories and rumors continue to this day. One theory, which became increasingly popular when war broke out in the Pacific, was that Amelia had really been on a spying mission and her plane had either crashed while she was carrying out this mission or she was captured by the Japanese. This seems unlikely, given all available evidence.

Instead, most researchers agree that Amelia was probably forced down somewhere within 100 miles (161 kilometers) of Howland Island. Clouds or the glare of the sun rising on the water may have made both the island and the *Itasca* nearby difficult to spot from the air. Amelia had been flying for 23 hours and fatigue and the stress of dwindling fuel supplies may have added to the difficulties. It seems most likely that she was unable to locate Howland Island before running out of fuel.

THE LEGACY

The contribution Amelia made to aviation extends beyond the milestones she set and the records she broke. Her "firsts," while impressive, are merely the starting point in an extra-ordinary life. The mystery surrounding her disappearance continues to inspire new research and new theories, but she is more than simply a famous aviator lost at sea.

Much of Amelia's success was due to her own hard work and determination. Many who observed her and instructed her in her earliest days of flying agreed that she was not a "natural." Flying did not come easily to her—her accomplishments were due more to hard work and perseverance than to her own natural gifts.

She overcame an ordinary background to pursue an excep-tional career. She made choices without regard for whether or not the task was something a woman could or should do. She would not have defined herself as a feminist; instead she simply

Amelia Earhart will always be remembered for her record-setting successes as a pilot and for her contributions to future aviators.

set goals for herself and sought opportunities without regard for whether or not women traditionally had achieved them. She was aware of her responsibility as a role model, and once she had built a career as a successful aviator, she encouraged other young women to fly. Her goals and accomplishments inspired other women to fly more, to fly faster, and to fly better.

The members of the first generation of aviators, both male and female, advanced the potential of aviation. Their search for new records to break, new "firsts" to achieve, demanded a new class of aircraft—faster, safer, and bigger. Airplane designers and developers were forced to keep up with these demands, and the ongoing push for more advanced, faster, and safer planes are a result of the efforts of early pioneers of aviation like Amelia Earhart.

1897   Amelia Earhart born on July 27 in Atchison, Kansas.

1917   Serves as military nurse in Canada for wounded World War I soldiers.

1920   Takes her first flight in California.

1921   Purchases her first airplane, a Kinner Airster.

1922   Sets unofficial women's flying altitude record at 14,000 feet (4,267 meters).

1925   Becomes a social worker in Boston.

1928   Becomes the first woman to fly across the Atlantic Ocean. Becomes the first woman to complete a transcontinental flight. Buys the Lockheed Vega. Finishes third in Women's Air Derby.

1931   Becomes the first president of the Ninety-Nines. Marries George Putnam. Sets women's autogiro altitude record at 18,415 feet (5,613 meters). Completes her first solo transcontinental flight in an autogiro. Becomes the first woman to fly solo across the Atlantic, and the first person to fly twice across the Atlantic. Sets women's record for fastest nonstop transcontinental flight (19 hours, 5 minutes).

1932   Breaks her own transcontinental record by flying across the United States in 17 hours, 7 minutes, and 30 seconds.

1935   First person to fly solo across the Pacific Ocean. First person to fly solo from Los Angeles to Mexico City. First woman to compete in National Air Races in Cleveland, Ohio.

1937   Begins first attempt at round-the-world flight in Oakland, California, and sets record for east-west (Oakland to Hawaii) travel in 15 hours, 47 minutes. Begins second attempt at round-the-world flight in Miami. Disappears near Howland Island.

Books

Backus, Jean L. *Letters from Amelia*. Boston, Ma.: Beacon Press, 1982.

Bell, Elizabeth S. *Sisters of the Wind*. Pasadena, Ca.: Trilogy Books, 1994.

Lomax, Judy. *Women of the Air*. New York: Dodd, Mead, 1987.

Lovell, Mary S. *The Sound of Wings*. New York: St. Martin's Press, 1989.

Moolman, Valerie. *Women Aloft*. Alexandria, Va.: Time-Life Books, 1981.

Putnam, George Palmer. *Soaring Wings*. New York: Harcourt, Brace & Co., 1939.

Rich, Doris L. *Amelia Earhart: A Biography*. Washington, D.C.: The Smithsonian Institution, 1989.

Websites

www.Ameliaearhart.com

www.Ameliaearhartmuseum.org

www.Foia.Fbi.gov/earhart

www.NASM.SI.edu

www.Ninety-nines.org

www.Smithsonian.org

Books

Butler, Susan. *East to Dawn: The Life of Amelia* Earhart. Cambridge, Ma.: Da Capo Press, 1999.

Goldstein, Donald M. and Katherine V. Dillon. *Amelia: The Centennial Biography of an Aviation Pioneer.* London: Chrysalis Books Ltd., 1997.

Gormley, Beatrice. *Amelia Earhart: Young Aviator.* New York: Aladdin Paperbacks, 2000.

Long, Elgen M. and Marie K. Long. *Amelia Earhart: The Mystery Solved.* New York: Simon & Schuster, 1999.

Ryan, Pam Munoz and Brian Selznick. *Amelia and Eleanor Go For a Ride.* New York: Scholastic Trade, 1999.

Websites

www.Ameliaearhart.com

Ameliaearhartmuseum.org

Greatamericanwomen.com

NASM.SI.edu

Ninety-nines.org

ABOUT THE AUTHOR

Heather Lehr Wagner is a writer and editor. She earned an M.A. from the College of William and Mary and a B.A. from Duke University. She has written several books for teens on global and family issues, and is also the author of *Charles Lindbergh* in the Famous Flyers series. She lives with her husband and their three children in Pennsylvania.